SERIAL KILLER

GROUPIES

by RJ PARKER

SERIAL KILLER

GROUPIES

by RJ PARKER

ISBN: 13- 978-1502540904
ISBN: 10- 1502540908

RJ Parker Publishing, Inc.
United States of America

Edited by: Hartwell Editing
Cover Design: Aeternum Designs

Contents

Acknowledgements

Firstly, this book is not meant to judge anyone. Most people have a fascination to something in their lives. We all slow down and rubberneck when we pass an accident because we are curious. It's that dark spot in our brains. Shows like "CSI," "Criminal Minds," "Cold Cases," and other true crime documentaries are very popular because we have a fascination with the criminal mind. There are rock star groupies, movie stars groupies, sports groupies, and even author groupies. For whatever reason, we choose to focus on something or someone, and despite what others may think, there's no difference between a serial killer groupie or any other type of groupie, in my opinion.

That being said, I thank my daughters Amanda and Katie for their ongoing support, despite that there are days I'm in too much pain to write. AS and Parkinson's are both getting worse all the time and typing is starting to become an issue. I hope I get to write another 16 more books, though.

Thanks to my editor and friend, Deb Hartwell, as well as Katherine McCarthy at Aeternum Designs, who designed this book cover.

And a very special thank you to my beta readers:

JoAnn Arden M. Brown
Melissa Dawn Risner Craft
Patricia Engebretsen-Lenckus
Kristal Grimsley-Baker
Kim Rael
Ron Steed
Diane White

Introduction

If you search for the definition of a 'groupie' in the common dictionary, you will come across a simple definition; it means a person, usually a woman, who is a regular follower of a pop music group, or any other celebrity. In simple terms, she likes the group and harbors hope of meeting them. Groupies are very common for music bands and celebrities; they follow them to different concerts and events, and they don't mind rendering their services to the group if needed. However, if applied broadly, the term 'groupie' could be used for a number of other purposes, for example, a serial killer groupie.

Serial killers, for the most part, live in plain sight, are active in their community, have a family, a house, a career, and typically blend in well. Many have an above average IQ. The motive for killing is not what many think, that of sexual gratification, but may vary from the thrill of the kill, feelings of control or anger, or the killer is simply seeking attention. The motive for most female serial killers is for financial gain.

According to the 1988 Congressional Law of the United States, a serial killer is a person who has killed three or more people, with a "cooling off" period. Many other sources, such as the Federal Bureau of Investigation, do not believe that there need to be a minimum of three murders committed by a person to be classified as a serial killer. The official description the Federal Bureau of Investigation determined at the 2005 Serial Murder Symposium[i] defines a serial killer as follows: 'a series of two or more murders, committed as separate events, usually, but not always, by one offender acting alone'.

Contrary to what many may think, serial killers aren't a new occurrence in society. Many people believe that serial killers became prominent in society during the latter years of the twentieth century, but that is just not true. In fact, this was simply the time when people began to focus on the news more, and law enforcement began to realize that the power of the media could be used to broadcast information regarding those who were harming the decorum of society.

It should be known that serial killing cannot be regarded as the same as spree killing or mass murdering; serial killers usually choose victims that share a similar set of traits, they usually kill to satiate their own desires, and they are often mentally deranged. Now that we have established who serial killers are and how they operate, let's turn our attention to serial killer groupies. These are people, again, quite commonly women (owing to the large majority of serial killers who are men), who actively follow serial killers, write to them, and communicate with them.

The funny thing is, just about every serial killer has a groupie attached to him or her. A cursory search on the internet for 'serial killer addresses' will result in a number of different addresses, a large majority of which are prison addresses. Many prison guards and officials have reported that a large amount of mail received by serial killers comes from groupies—women who just want to communicate with them, even though they have had no prior association with these individuals. In November of 2012, I interviewed Paul Bernardo, known as the **Scarborough Rapist or the Schoolgirl Killer, who is serving out his life sentence** in Ontario. I was told by the warden that Bernardo still receives a couple hundred love letters every month, a far cry from several hundred a week when he was first arrested with his wife, Karla Homolka.

Again, serial killer groupies are not a new phenomenon; they have been around for hundreds of years. One of the most obvious cases that comes to mind is that of William Henry Theodore Durrant, one of the earliest serial killers to be documented in America. William Henry Theodore Durrant was a superintendent of Sunday School at the Emmanuel Baptist Church, as well as a doctor in training at the Cooper Medical College situated in San Francisco.

Perhaps you can gauge his animalistic nature from the fact that he was referred to as 'The Demon of Belfry.' On the face of it, Henry William Theodore Durrant was just like any other man; polite, well dressed, and handsome. He had an aura of innocence surrounding him, and Durrant was often quite awkward in his behavior, acting shy most of the time. But this is no unusual occurrence amongst men.

Durrant's first killing was Blanche Lamont, a twenty-year-old girl whom he was dating, who disappeared after the couple was last seen walking into church together one afternoon in 1895. Soon after the disappearance of Blanche Lamont, Durrant was seen again with another young woman, Minnie Williams, who also disappeared. The two women's bodies were found a short time later in the church—they had both suffered the same fate. The women had been mutilated and raped, possibly pre- and postmortem. After the police found the bodies, a search ensued and Durrant was captured. His three-week trial became an international sensation; many news agencies were there to cover the trial and several newspapers allotted their front-page headlines to the story.

However, his trial also surprised a great many people for one thing—the sheer number of women who flocked to the courthouse to catch a glimpse of the handsome killer. Many of the female reporters were also quick to make notes about the silly behavior that the women exhibited, expressing embarrassment at their gender's representation. As was reported, the front row of the gallery was occupied solely by women who wanted to get a look at the killer, and when the coffins of the two victims had been laid out, many of the women were willing to get in line twice in order to get a proper look. The horrific nature of the behavior at the time represented the moral decay of society, but it was just the beginning of a long-standing trend in the history of American crime. Rather than inspiring horror and repulsion from women, this serial killer actually inspired devotion, curiosity, and even romantic love in some women.

At the time, one woman stood out from the rest, and even achieved status as a minor celebrity. Harold Schecter, author of *The Serial Killer Files*,[ii] noted that blonde Rosalind Bowers would attend the trial each morning, carrying a bouquet of sweet pea flowers. She would send these flowers to Durrant, and in one appearance, Durrant was even spotted sporting one of those flowers in his lapel. It came to the point that Bowers even tried to see Durrant in his cell, but he refused to grant her appearance. Regardless, she would appear in court at every session in a dutiful manner, and it didn't take very long for the press to pick up on her unusual gesture. While writing her book, *Sympathy for the Devil,* Virginia A. McConnell documented the incident.

Bowers was soon widely referred to as the 'Sweet Pea Girl,' and she became a point of attention for the massive crowds that would gather at the courthouse. People would flock to the courthouse to see if she would make an appearance in court and perform the same ritual each day. One of the reporters even got a seat next to her, and noted all of her melodramatic poses and gestures throughout the day as the court continued its proceedings. It didn't take very long for people to realize that Bowers was someone who badly needed attention. Additionally, word soon came that Bowers was a married woman, and when her husband learned of her activities, he was, obviously, enraged.

Did Bowers want to help Durrant gain the sympathy of the jury? Did she simply want attention for herself? Or, did she just want to connect with Durrant? Was it something more personal? It does not matter what her motives were; her actions brought about a completely different dimension to the trial. The moralists of that era were quick to view the excessive amount of female attention that Durrant received as reason enough to argue that women should not even be allowed to hear such details at all. Despite all the attention that Durrant received, and the hilarious efforts of the defense attorney to pin the blame of the murders on the church's pastor, it didn't take very long for the all-male jury to convict the young doctor in training of both murders, and a recommendation for the death penalty was put forth. On January 7, 1898, William Henry Theodore Durrant was hanged at San Quentin prison. Throughout the entire time that he was on death row, Durrant claimed that he was innocent.

Rosalind Bowers, or the Sweet Pea Girl, as she was now known to the media, disappeared amongst the many pages of history, but her peculiar obsession with Durrant associated her with a certain group of people, mostly women, who flock to trials and prisons, even to this day, in order to gain the attention of brutal murderers and crazed killers. Known as 'serial killer groupies,' or even 'prison groupies' by some, a great number of these women have shown a surprising desire to connect with a serial killer of their choice. Many of these women have become directly aligned with these killers, and some have even married, or gotten engaged with these criminals.

It is believed that these women are living vicariously through these high profile criminals and enjoy the attention and notoriety in the media. Like many other mental conditions, treatment for such a condition varies from medications, such as Phenothiazine, to psychotherapy.

So why are these so-called 'groupies' attracted to serial killers? Experts have compiled several reasons why, including:

1. *Rescue fantasy.* The groupie believes that he or she can change the killer with love and understanding.
2. *Perfect boyfriend/girlfriend.* The groupie knows where his or her criminal lover is at all times (in prison). She can love him without being jealous or having to deal with trust issues.
3. *Nurturing.* Most female groupies have said that they see the little boy in these serial killers and that they want to console and nurture them like a mother would do with her son.
4. *Drama.* Many women and men need to have drama in their lives. They become engrossed in the trial of a serial killer, then an infatuation begins, which leads to sending letters to the killer.
5. *Hybristophilia.* Some people experience sexual arousal by being with someone who commits violent crimes.
6. *Male figure.* Several female groupies have acknowledged that they were raised without a father figure in their

life. Abused and neglected, they look to the serial killer to fill that need.

7. *Self-esteem.* Some women have very low self-esteem and believe that they can't find a man. Since these killers are in prison and lonely themselves, those women will target them for attention and a fantasy relationship.

8. *Attention seeking.* When the media places a killer in the spotlight, groupies will often get involved to draw attention to themselves.

9. *Beauty and the Beast Syndrome.* Groupies will align themselves with a serial killer to get close to the danger—not enough to get hurt, but enough to feel the fear.

These groupies will do almost anything to get close to the prisoner that they are attracted to. They give up their jobs, family, spend money on him, and even move across country to be in the same town as him. Most SKGs are attractive and well educated. Many are already married; they are mothers, and in several cases, they even work in law enforcement or psychology.

They sometimes wait for hours just to have a few minutes every week or so to have a face-to-face visit in the prison. It is worthy to note that a large number of these SKGs were raised in a Catholic home and were struck by the church's teachings on sexism, repressions of sexuality, and subjugation of women in general. Many of them grew up without a father, abused and withdrawn.

Some SKGs are attracted to the celebrity status they acquire. They go on talk shows to announce their undying love for the serial killer and proclaim that he was not capable of these killings. Or, that he has changed. Some have even taken credit for 'changing' the killer.

Paul Bernardo is incarcerated at the Kingston Maximum Prison in Ontario Canada after being convicted of three murders from 1990 to 1992, as well as multiple rapes and sexual assaults. He was known as the Scarborough Rapist and the Schoolgirl Killer. His wife at the time, Karla Homolka, was convicted of manslaughter pursuing a plea bargain in the 1991 and 1992 rape and murders of two Ontario young teenage girls, Kristen French and Leslie Mahaffy, and later the rape and murder of her own sister, Tammy Homolka.

Both Bernardo and Homolka were arrested in 1993. In 1995, Bernardo was convicted and received life in prison, as Canada doesn't have the death penalty. In 1993, Homolka claimed that her husband abused her and that she was an unwilling participant to the rapes and murders. She struck a deal with the prosecutors for a reduced prison sentence of twelve years in exchange for a guilty plea to manslaughter. Videotapes filmed during the crimes later revealed that Homolka was actually an active participant. However, the deal had already been signed and the prosecutors received a black eye in the media, who dubbed it the "deal with the devil." She was released from prison in 2005 and falls under the category of an aggressive hybristophile.

In the next chapter, we'll explore hybristophilia further.

Hybristophilia

Hybristophilia is technically described as a "paraphilia of the predatory type in which a person can be sexually aroused, or even achieve orgasm in response to, or contingent upon, being with a partner who is known to have committed an outrage, like cheating or lying, or known infidelities of crime, such as rape, murder or armed robbery." Many people refer to hybristophilia as the 'Bonnie and Clyde Syndrome.' And, in the context of this discussion, hybristophilia is an extremely important term. A great number of criminals, especially those who have committed heinous crimes, receive what you would call fan mail in prison, most of which are amorous, or even sexual in nature. It is presumed that this fan mail is written by those who are suffering from the Bonnie and Clyde Syndrome.

By now, you might be wondering why women are willing to go to such lengths in order to converse with such people. Many speculations have been bandied around, though no definite claim has risen. A professor of forensic psychology at DeSales University, Katherine Ramsland[iii] created a small set of reasons that are most often given by women who have married or dated serial killers at some point in their lives. Here are a few of them:

- **"They believe they can change a man as cruel and powerful as a serial killer."** Many women have stated that one of the primary reasons that they are willing to marry or date a serial killer is because they harbor an opinion inside their minds that they will be able to change the man, and remove his cruel habits. They believe that they can make him fall in love with them, ultimately gaining control.
- **"Some 'see' the little boy that the killer once was and seek to find and nurture him."** One of the most common reasons given by women who date serial killers is the fact that they 'see' the little boy that the horrible man once used to be, and they believe that they can nurture that kid, hence removing the cruel and harmful nature of the killer and making him amicable again.
- **"They craved the attention of the media, and hoped to land a book or a movie deal."** Several women also

claimed that they hoped to share in the attention that the media afforded to these serial killers, and were hoping that any news agency or a publication house would be willing to offer them a book or movie deal. This is quite common, as many wives of serial killers have managed to land book deals in order to share their experiences with the public at large. Unfortunately, with the media's crackdown on serial killers, many channels have decided not to provide undue attention to the heinous criminals. Such book deals are becoming more and more scarce.

- **"The perfect boyfriend."** Another important reason that many women give is the fact that the serial killer is the 'perfect boyfriend.' She has a clear idea of where he is at all times (prison, of course!) and also knows that he is going to be thinking about her. Hence, she is able to easily claim that her boyfriend loves her. More importantly, she doesn't have to worry about the many different daily issues that individuals in normal relationships face. For instance, she doesn't have to cook for him, wash his clothes, or be accountable to him. She can do what she wants and go where she wants, without bothering about him at all, or even letting him know. And, she knows where he will be at all times. What more could a girlfriend ask for? According to Katherine Ramsland, the woman can keep this fantasy charged up for quite a long while.

Apart from these, one of the reasons that have been offered by mental experts is that many women who feel affectionate towards serial killers are suffering from an extreme form of fanaticism. Mental experts state that these women are unable to find love in normal life, and hence look for it within other outlets, such as these individuals whom society has shunned. Ultimately, they look for relationships that they know cannot be consummated.

Several other psychologists who focus upon evolutionary psychology, such as Leon F. Seltzer, have given slightly different reasons. In his view, serial killers are regarded as alpha males—powerful, lethal, and able to break the rules—and, as a result, they are able to easily attract women. He said the reason why women are attracted towards these individuals is the fact that throughout evolutionary history, such men were known for protecting their women, as well as their offspring.

Nowadays, even though women have a conscious understanding that they must not become romantically involved with a serial killer, they still find themselves attracted to the killers because, as Seltzer writes, "As a therapist I've encountered many women who bemoaned their vulnerability towards dominant men who, consciously, they recognized were all wrong for them." Throughout history, there have been countless examples of women who have been attracted to serial killers, several cases of which shall be discussed in this book.

In linguistic terms, a woman who loves or dates a criminal is known as a hybristophile. Hybristophilia has two distinct types: passive and aggressive hybristophilia. **Passive hybristophilia** is when a person is willing to contact a serial killer after hearing about them from the media, or any other sources. **Aggressive hybristophilia** is when a woman is actively involved in the crime, along with the instigator himself. In passive hybristophilia, women usually need a response from the criminal that they have tried to contact, and once they get a response, they begin to create an imaginary love affair in their minds and hearts, which continues until it is completely broken by the criminal himself, sometimes even after.

Some women remain under the impression that to commit such heinous crimes is the ultimate expression of masculinity. Usually, before initiating contact with such criminals, women are apprehensive; they don't know how he will respond. More often than not, after the first meeting, the women are pleasantly surprised at the ordinary behavior of the criminal and his expression of humanity, as well as the level of respect that he shows in his communication. In the case of psychopaths, the charm exhibited by the criminals also plays a major role. These men usually have very ordinary habits; some will like dogs, others will prefer cats, some will have very common hobbies, like cooking or gardening, which makes them seem not too different from the ordinary person. Some of these criminals even have special talents to their name. Add to the fact that most of these criminals are known for their good looks—that is how they lure these women into their traps—and a love story begins to take shape within the woman's mind.

Professor John Money,[iv] a prominent sexologist, described hybristophilia as a sexual paraphilia in which a person is able to attain sexual arousal or pleasure from a sexual partner that is known to have "committed an outrage or a crime, such as rape, murder, or armed robbery." As mentioned earlier, many often refer to it as the Bonnie and Clyde Syndrome. Why? There's a deeper reference here— Bonnie Elizabeth Parker and Clyde Chestnut Barrow were famous outlaws in America who hailed from the Dallas area and traveled throughout the United States with their gang during the times of the Great Depression. They carried out dozens of bank robberies, and were even known to have robbed a huge number of small stores as well as rural gas stations. Their exploits were soon known throughout the American countryside, and even though both were killed at the young age of twenty-five and twenty-four in 1934, their exploits became renowned across the globe. Perhaps it can be said that their reputation was revived and cemented in American history forever by the 1967 film, *Bonnie and Clyde*, directed by Arthur Penn. The film starred Faye Dunaway and Warren Beatty, and it showed how two people, both of whom committed serious crimes, were attracted to each other as a result of their actions.

In most cases, the hybristophile's focus of sexual desire (the criminal) is someone who has been imprisoned. In other cases, the hybristophile might even coax the criminal to commit a crime so as to derive sexual pleasure out of it. Similarly, many hybristophiles write to imprisoned criminals, whom they do not know on a personal level, but are only aware of due to the attention given to them by the media.

Many of the high profile serial killers and murderers that have passed throughout the pages of history, such as Ted Bundy, Charles Manson, Richard Ramirez, and Jeffrey Dahmer, were famous for the sheer amount of female attention and fan mail that they received in prison, both during and after their trials. In a book chapter review written by Corey Vitello in 2006, he stated that contrary to the most common paraphilic behaviors, hybristophilia is slightly different due to the fact that it is more common amongst females rather than men, and "that it varies in both disposition and degree." Simply put, passive hybristophilia is when a hybristophile has no intention of committing the crime herself, but derives sexual pleasure from a partner who commits such crimes. However, aggressive hybristophilia is when a person actively participates in committing the crime, and derives sexual pleasure from it as well.

The website of *Love Art History*[v] claims that "these women are usually delusional and will try to find excuses for what the criminal did. They will develop relationships with a criminal and feel that they are special—that even though their lover may have killed numerous people, he would never harm her. They usually feel that they can 'change' their lover and have rescue *fantasies.* Passive hybristophiliacs tend to put themselves in positions to be seduced, manipulated, and lied to by the people they fall for."

As for aggressive hybristophiles, the website claims that these women "help out their lovers with their criminal agenda by luring victims, hiding bodies, covering crimes, or even committing crimes. They are attracted to their lovers because of their violent actions and want to receive love, yet are unable to understand that their lovers are psychopaths who are manipulating them. Both passive and aggressive hybristophiliacs tend to end up in abusive or unhealthy relationships."

The reasons that have been put forth for hybristophilia are highly speculative. Corey Vitello writes (cited from *The Thrill of the*

Killer, by Cara Bruce): "Women, teens especially, have the unfortunate reputation for wanting to find a partner who fits the 'bad boy image.' The sexy bad boy is a staple American icon. He embodies machismo, individualism and all that other... potent ideals of the U.S. Bad boys come in differing degrees, and most women would confess to having a minor crush on at least one at the end of the spectrum... Maybe, women fall for the bad boys because they are forbidden. Perhaps it's the ultimate taboo, thus, the ultimate aphrodisiac. Consequently, those women who do not grow out of the bad-boy fixation become a hybristophile because the image is so strongly paired with sexual arousal; they need to be with a notorious partner to achieve sexual pleasure."

Evolutionary psychologists believe that these females have some kind of unconscious biological drive that makes them feel that these men have a greater chance of survival. A great number of hybristophiles have submissive traits, and as the *Love Art History* website states, are "narcissist enablers who are attracted to power." Professor John Money claims that the behavior may be caused due to an issue of a reverse operant conditioning. He says that the "opponent process converts negative into positive, tragedy into triumph, and aversion into addiction. Two recreational examples of opponent process reversals are bungee jumping and riding a gravity defying roller coaster. The novice whose apprehension amounts to sheer terror at first may, after very few trials, discover that terror transmogrifies into exhilaration and ecstasy, as if the *brain* had released a flood of its own opiate-like endorphins. Thereafter, the thrill returns with each repeat, totally replacing terror."

According to Sheila Isenberg, who interviewed a great number of hybristophiles in the course of writing her book, *Women Who Love Men Who Kill*,[vi] stated that while some of the hybristophiles agreed that they knew the relationship was morally wrong, many others were described as being delusional, with idealized fantasies. Many of the hybristophiles she interviewed were individuals who were living ordinary lives with ordinary jobs, such as nurses and teachers, though a great number of them had been with partners who were abusive and violent towards them. Hybristophiles know that the male is in jail; hence they have a sense of security that they never had before regarding this situation. Now the woman is able to feel that she is in control. She can do what she wants without having to bother about the man himself. Additionally, she is not accountable to him for anything.

Academically, this confirms the view of many sexologists and psychologists that hybristophiles are generally those who have very low self-esteem, do not think very highly of themselves, and are often the subject of violence and abuse. Ultimately, the feelings that these women have are easily mistaken by them for love, as they also contain serious sexual attraction (many women have confirmed that they tend to masturbate and orgasm after reading about and talking to these serial killers). Importantly, this feeling of love is never really contradicted by reality—since the two do not live together, and only ever meet in prison (on very rare occasions), the relationship turns out to be perfect for a delusional person who has idealized fantasies. This is the ultimate reality-proof romance, where the dreams are shaped by the person and never contradicted by the truth.

The hybristophile begins to think of herself as being somebody special. She thinks that she is the only one who can understand his pain; she thinks that even though he has managed to kill a number of people, he wouldn't harm her. Even if the evidence is clear as day that he is a criminal, she will concoct up stories and beliefs that tend to mitigate the truth. Some believe that they can change the person or rescue him from his current state. Underneath all of this, the female will have an extremely erotic lust for the man.

Now that we have established the primary reasons regarding what causes hybristophilia, it is important to talk about some of the most popular cases of hybristophilia. We have already talked about Rosalind Bowers, and how she was such a major attraction for the media because of the expression of affection that she showed towards Theodore Durrant. I'll cover several others next.

Carol Anne Boone

Carol Anne Boone was the wife of probably one of the most notorious killers in the history of the United States of America. You read that right—*wife*. Ted Bundy, whom we shall talk about later on in this book, was hardly the person any woman would perceive as her 'Mr. Right,' especially considering the fact that he was arrested on suspicions of being connected to more than thirty brutal murders, all of them women who were found with their bodies mutilated and mangled, sometimes even cut up into pieces, and discarded in the Pacific Northwestern region.

There's a lot more detail that we will delve into later when talking about Ted Bundy, but Carol Anne Boone has to be one of the most hardcore serial killer groupies out there. She even decided to move to Florida in order to be closer and to marry Ted Bundy. Their love and affection could be gauged from the fact that Bundy managed to get her pregnant, even though all kinds of conjugal visits were ostensibly forbidden within the high security prison where Bundy was kept.

They had a daughter together. However, by the time Bundy was executed in 1989, Carol

Anne Boone had divorced him by that point, and had taken their daughter and fled the state. Her current whereabouts are unknown as yet, and even though the marriage lasted merely three years, it does go on to show the level of commitment that these groupies are willing to put on the line. While she maintains a low profile nowadays, her life was in the news virtually every day when she was in touch with Ted Bundy.

Charles Watson, one of the most notorious serial killers of his time, was also featured popularly in the news for something other than killing—his marriage with twenty-year-old Kristin Svege. He had been corresponding with her for quite some time before she moved to San Luis Obispo, California, at Watson's behest. Just so you know, Charles 'Tex' Watson was the only male person present that night in 1969 when five people, along with an unborn child, were brutally murdered at 1005 Cielo Drive, in Benedict Canyon, California. Many people considered him to be the right hand man of Charles Manson.

It came to the point that Charles Watson became a born again Christian in prison, and even became an ordained minister by the year 1983. Ultimately, the court allowed Watson and Kristin to celebrate their honeymoon in a trailer that was situated on the grounds of the California Men's Colony in San Luis Obispo and, along with the numerous conjugal visits that Kristin would undertake during his time in prison, she managed to give birth to four of his children. The marriage ended in an annulment in the year 2003. But, rather than leaving him for another man, the reason that Kristin gave was that "some of his actions in prison were not becoming of a person whom he claimed to be."

Either way, the decision was not at all easy for Kristin Svege, and she struggled with the consequences of her actions for several years afterwards. She also began to understand the impact that her decision was having on her children. There are a lot of unconfirmed details that can be used to connect the dots from then till the present, but as they are not confirmed, mere speculation is not fit to be included in this book. She is currently married to another man and all of her children are doing very well, according to her. Funnily enough, Kristin raised all of her children herself, via home schooling and tutoring methods, and they are all devout Christians.

The last example that we shall discuss before moving on with the details of the serial killers and the attention that they draw is the case of Carol Spadoni, the wife of Philip Carl Jablonski. To put things in context, Carol met and married Philip while he was serving twelve years in San Quentin Prison for the brutal murder of his former wife. When Philip Carl Jablonski was released on parole, Carol Spadoni spoke directly to the parole officer. She told him about the fear she harbored from Philip Jablonski, and that it was not such a good idea to have him living with her and her mother. Jablonski was released anyway. He committed several criminal acts during parole, but the bottom line is the fact that Jablonski also murdered Carol Spadoni.

It doesn't matter what led her to him in the first place; the only thing to consider here is that she was murdered by her husband, who was already a notorious serial killer. Carol Spadoni died a gruesome death, and even though Jablonski was captured again, and was even sentenced to death (he's still in prison), she lost her life for someone that she wanted to be with.

There are numerous other cases that we will talk about during the course of this book, including the lives and actions of different serial killers, along with their groupies (including notable names), to give you an idea of what really attracted these serial killer groupies to them in the first place.

Serial Killer with a Conscience?
Wayne Adam Ford

Twenty-nine-year-old Patricia Anne Tamez was living a life that was like a rocking boat. Tamez could usually be found lumbering her way through the streets, looking for a quick fix, or in search of potential customers to whom she could prostitute her body in order to sustain her drug habit. When she couldn't be found on the streets, it was highly likely that she would be in a state hospital or a mental institution undergoing rigorous drug rehabilitation and psychiatric therapy. During her college years, Tamez had been a popular, vivacious individual. However, hard times befell her, and soon her motives and ambitions changed; her only ambition was now to ensure that her drug habit could be sustained.

On October 22, 1998, Patricia Anne Tamez spent the earlier parts of the day prostituting and soliciting sex from truck drivers near the intersection of 6th and D streets in Victorville, California. She had been trying for quite a few hours, but to little avail, until a large sized, jet-black truck pulled up near her and gave her a proposition. The conversation was pretty brief, and Tamez realized that this man was willing to pay her. That man was Wayne Ford.

Wayne Adam Ford was born on December 3, 1961, in the town of Petaluma, California. He was the second son of an American father, while his mother was an immigrant from Germany. Like many serial killers, Wayne Adam Ford did not have a very good childhood. His parents were constantly fighting, and by the time he had turned ten years old, they had already divorced. During high school, Wayne realized that he wasn't up to the task of studying, so he instead enlisted in the U.S. Marine Corps, serving for six years and taking an honorable discharge in 1985. Despite his unhappy childhood, for most of his life he was a relatively stable young man. Unfortunately, his psyche began to suffer in 1983 and he underwent serious psychological declines, which ultimately resulted in significant problems at his work place. He was also hospitalized on several occasions during this period of time.

He married twice during this period, both of which ended in a divorce. This was also the first time that Wayne Adam Ford began to disobey the law. He was alleged to have beaten and robbed a prostitute at one point. He also used cruel punishment on animals, and he even suffered a brief jail sentence for his actions towards animals. At the time of his arrest, Wayne Adam Ford was employed as a long-haul truck driver. So far, it is difficult to really understand what might have led him towards killing.

Prostitution and sex solicitation are both businesses that come with a lot of risks; the woman has to get in the car of a completely unknown stranger, who then takes her to a completely unknown place, while she has to hope that he will keep the original arrangement and pay her as she deserves. Unfortunately, it doesn't always pan out that way. In the case of Patricia Anne Tamez, October 22, 1998 was the last time she was ever going to get into a truck with a man and drive off in the hopes of getting some payment later on.

Later that evening, a couple of security guards at the California Aqueduct were patrolling by when they saw what appeared to be a silhouette bobbing within the water. They were confused at first; the rolling water near the pump house was churning at a rapid pace, and it was difficult to make out what that strange shape was. As they pulled closer, they saw, much to their horror, the shape of a human body. Without hesitance, one of the guards placed a call to the police.

Upon arrival, the authorities were quick to pull the nude body from the water. Imagine the horror and shock that must have befallen the authorities when they found out that one of the woman's breasts had been completely severed off. It was clear to all of the officers and guards present at the scene that she had been murdered, brutally too. An autopsy was carried out later on, and it was found that she had been subjected to severe trauma just before her death. Clear evidence was found that she had been tightly bound, raped, and had also been hit directly on the head with blunt force. Additionally, her attacker had completely broken her back, and had cut off one of her breasts *before* he had strangled her. The pain and terror she must have felt cannot possibly be translated into words. It didn't take long to determine that these were the remains of one Patricia Anne Tamez, who had gone missing from the corner of 6th and D streets.

A search was conducted of the area where Tamez's body was found, and during that search, up the stream from the aqueduct, the police found a host of different items that created a strong link with the murder—a towel that was stained red with blood, pants, a blouse and a .22 caliber air pistol. Her missing breast was nowhere to be found, nor did the police have any leads on the horrific murderer who had carried out such a gruesome act. It only took a couple of weeks for the detectives to get a massive break in the case.

On November 3 in the same year, a long-haul trucker by the name of Wayne Adam Ford walked into the Sheriff's Department of Humboldt County, situated in Eureka, California. His brother, Rod, had spent the previous day persuading him to turn himself in, and it seemed he'd finally relented. A short while after arriving at the police station, Wayne Adam Ford broke down in tears and confessed out loud that he had murdered four women. In his pocket was a plastic bag, which was fished out when the authorities immediately began to frisk him. The plastic bag contained a severed breast, which the authorities were able to link with Patricia Anne Tamez later on.

Many writers, scholars, and criminologists have been baffled by the actions of Wayne Adam Ford. For instance, in his book, *Shadows of Evil*, Carlton Smith explains that the probability of a serial killer turning himself in is usually extremely low. These serial killers feel no remorse for their actions, so it was amazing for most to see that Ford had not only turned himself in, but also seemed to feel genuine remorse for his actions. A criminologist working for the San Francisco State University, Mike Rustigan wrote in an article for the *Associated Press* that the confessions given by Wayne Adam Ford were "truly an exception in the annals of serial killers." Because of the shameful confession that he had just given to the police, Wayne Adam Ford was quickly dubbed as the "serial killer with a conscience."

Unfortunately, as the police began to investigate the murders to which Wayne was linked, they soon found that it was unlikely that he had even the slightest bit of guilt. The brutal nature of the murders that he had carried out, considering the torture and the manner in which the women had been murdered, made it clear that this was a man devoid of any conscience at all. The police also came to the conclusion that had Ford not turned himself in, the probability of him killing again was very high; it was clear that his violent passion was very much out of control.

According to an *Associated Press* article, Wayne had also worked as a chemical and biological specialist during his time in the U.S.

Marine Corps. It was made clear that Wayne took his job very seriously and had wanted to further his rank. During his employment, Wayne Ford married a woman he had known for a brief amount of time. The article, written by Jeff Barnard, stated soon after the wedding, Wayne became increasingly obsessive and demanding, and would often abuse her. Eventually, the strain on their marriage became too much, and the couple divorced.

While it is often stated that Wayne was honorably discharged from the U.S. Marine Corps, an article written by Rick Halperin on the website *Death Penalty News-California* revealed that he had been let go due to suffering from serious mental problems. By 1994, Wayne was dating a nineteen-year-old girl, with whom he had gotten in touch with while working at a karaoke bar as a singer. The courtship didn't last very long; the relationship soon turned into a marital bond and she soon became pregnant. However, like many relationships that existed in Wayne's world, this one soon began to crack as well.

Five months into her pregnancy, she and Wayne had a dispute, after which he raped her. The incident was a horrific experience for the poor teen, and left a permanent mark on her.

The nature of his horrific actions was further compounded by the fact that he was completely indifferent to what he had done. She took leave and moved with her mother in Las Vegas. They soon patched things up and she moved back in with Wayne. Their on-and-off relationship would continue until after the birth of their child in 1995.

Wayne suffered from severe psychosis during the course of this relationship, and he would often make demands for his wife to participate in disturbing sexual fantasies of his, such as sleeping with unknown men while he would watch and stick needles into her breasts. Wayne also demanded that she keep the house clean, cook three meals a day, and care for the baby. She dutifully agreed, but regardless of how hard she worked, it was just never enough for Wayne, who continued to criticize her.

Wayne was also suffering from severe bouts of depression and, like in previous relationships, he became extremely controlling and abusive towards his wife. To her credit, his wife tried everything in her power to please him, but there was unfortunately very little that she could do in the first place. Even the little baby wasn't enough to save the marriage from falling into the abyss. Soon after the child was born, the couple divorced, and his wife and young child moved back in with her mother in Las Vegas. Wayne Adam Ford then took up permanent residence within a trailer home in Arcata, California.

After the divorce, Wayne made several complaints to authorities that he was denied visitation rights to his child. According to an article written by Rick Halperin, his wife stated that Wayne would "hurt him badly." Wayne's anger and abuse, which was already fueled due to the excessive amounts of alcohol that he drank, eventually turned deadly.

On October 26, 1997, a duck hunter was canoeing on the Ryan Slough near the Eureka River when his eyes fell upon an object that closely resembled a well-made mannequin near the muddy banks of the river. As he got closer to the silhouette sprawled on the muddy bank, shock and horror took over his senses as he began to realize that these were the butchered and mutilated remains of a woman, whose head, arms, and legs were nowhere to be found. The hunter was carrying a mobile phone and was quick to call the Humboldt County Police.[vii] As authorities arrived on the scene, they saw that the victim's body had been cut down the middle and had been completely disemboweled. Apart

41

from that, her breasts had been cut off, and there were approximately thirty stab wounds on the woman's body. Her arms were missing, so the authorities were unable to recover any fingerprints. Moreover, her head was missing and she didn't have any unusual markings or tattoos. As a result, investigators were unable to determine the woman's identity.

Hence, the woman was subsequently referred to as Jane Doe. The coroner determined that she was between the ages of eighteen and twenty-five, and had dark skin. It was also found that she had died three to four days before her body had been discovered. Approximately three months after her autopsy, one of her arms and her hand was found lying near a beach. However, the condition of her body parts had deteriorated to such an extent that it was nigh impossible to carry out a fingerprint analysis. Investigators came to the conclusion that it was likely her identity might never be discovered at all.

Fast forward to June of 1998, and another body was found floating in the California Aqueduct, this time near the town of Buttonwillow. The remains were taken to the Kern County Coroner's Office for a thorough examination, and the autopsy revealed that the woman had likely died as a result of being strangled. It was also clear that she had been raped and murdered several days before her body was discovered. This time however, the coroner was able to recover fingerprints from the victim, which were handed over to the police for identification. One month later, a match for the print was found. As per the information given in an article written by Glenn Puit for *Review-Journal*, the woman was singled out to be twenty-six-year-old Tina Renee Gibbs, a native of Tacoma, Washington. She had been working as a street prostitute prior to disappearing completely.

Months later, on September 25, police found the nude remains of another woman, this time lying near an irrigation ditch that had been dug out on the roadside off Interstate 5, near Lodi, California. A number of items were found near the body, all of which were thought to be connected to the murder— women's clothing, hair samples, a tarp that was stained red with blood, a plastic bag that bore a logo from a truck stop called 'Flying J,' along with a few articles of jewelry. Investigators hoped that these items would provide some clues that would lead them to the identity of the girl.

All this time, police were picking up on a pattern that seemed to be emerging. The mutilated remains of the women were found in obscure locations, not too frequently visited, but they were still locations where an occasional passerby might find the body. An autopsy was carried out on the latest victim, which provided information that the woman had been dead for numerous days, indicated by the advanced stage of decomposition. A puncture mark was also present on one of the woman's breasts, and evidence was found that the woman had been suffocated. Investigators came to the conclusion that the woman had been thrown from a moving vehicle into the ditch. Fingerprints revealed that the woman was twenty-five-year-old Lanette White, who'd hailed from Fontana, California. She had been seen last by her cousin as she left to get groceries in order to prepare milk for her baby. Nobody imagined that she would be found mutilated and murdered.

Soon after White's murder, Wayne called his brother, who immediately jumped to his aid. Wayne told him of the horrible acts that he had committed, and his brother, Rod, was quick to convince him to turn himself in. Wayne hadn't told Rod about the extent of injuries or murders that he had committed; he just told Rod that he had hurt some people. Wayne gave himself to the authorities the subsequent day.

While he was in the custody of the police, Wayne Adam Ford confessed to the murders of Patricia Anne Tamez, Tina Gibbs, Lanette White, as well as the woman who was yet unidentified and whose remains were found near the banks of Ryan Slough. At the time he committed these murders, Wayne Adam Ford was a long-haul truck driver and was carrying lumber throughout the areas of Oregon, California, Arizona and Nevada. He would usually abduct and rape his victims during these times. According to an article that was written by Bhavna Mistry in 1998 in the *Daily News*, Wayne's killing rampage was mainly sparked by the anger that he harbored for his ex-wife, whom he blamed for keeping his son away from him. The article also provided a crucial insight into his actions, stating that the primary reason he turned himself in was because he was "scared that he would kill his ex-wife, and he did not want his own son to be an orphan."

But, even though he had confessed to the murders, what about the evidence? Well, Wayne provided the police with the locations of where he'd buried the dismembered remains of the women he had murdered. For instance, he claimed that he'd buried the head and arms of the unidentified woman near the Mad River in northern California. The remaining parts, including her thighs, were kept in a freezer before he decided to bury them at a Trinidad campsite.

Investigators traveled to the Mad River in search of the head and arms of the unidentified woman, though they were unable to find anything. This further reduced the chances of the victim being identified. However, they were able to find the campsite where he had buried the body parts of Jane Doe. Further information regarding the nature of the murders was revealed by Wayne Adam Ford during the police investigations.

A thorough search was carried out on the trailer where Wayne had taken up permanent residence. In the kitchen, they found a coffee can that was believed to have contained the breast of Jane Doe. Similarly, they also found a plastic bag that had the same 'Flying J' logo on it as the one that had been found near the mutilated remains of Lanette White's body. All of the possessions found within the campsite were taken up to the police lab for further examination, along with Wayne's pickup truck. Even though the killer had presented himself to the authorities on a silver platter, they wanted to make sure that he was the one; they wanted to leave nothing to chance.

On November 6, 1998, Wayne Adam Ford was arraigned at the Superior Court of Humboldt County. Only one charge of first-degree murder was levied on him, even though he himself had confessed to murdering four women. The only charge against him was for the murder of Jane Doe. The other murders did not take place in the jurisdiction of Humboldt County Court. As a result, Wayne would have to be tried in the jurisdictions where the other murders had been committed.

During the trial proceedings, a large number of women were present in court to view the killer. Wayne made a formal complaint to Judge Bruce Watson that he did not have a lawyer, and the court confirmed the appointment of Kevin Robinson in order to defend Wayne. Immediately upon appointment, Robinson put forth a not guilty plea on behalf of Wayne Ford, his new client.

A number of other complicated trials took place around this time, and two months later after the arraignment of Wayne Ford, a new serial killer law was enacted, which gave prosecutors the power to combine all of the murders that had been committed into a singular trial. By doing so, Ford would not have to be tried in different counties for the murders that he had committed. He would instead stand trial for all four murders at once in San Bernardino County. Ford was facing the prospect of the death penalty. In August of the same year, he was transferred over to the West Valley Detention Center, which is situated in San Bernardino County, where he continued to await his upcoming trial.

The prosecutors and the defense were divided over whether the confessions given by Wayne Adam Ford should be admissible in court or not. It would be five long years before Ford finally stood trail.

In January of 2004, Superior Court Judge Michael Smith ruled that Ford's confessions were admissible at the trial. By then, Wayne Adam Ford had accumulated a number of public admirers, including a great deal of women, who would attend the court proceedings in the hopes of catching a glimpse of this handsome man. However, nobody had anticipated that the woman who would grab the headlines would not be amongst the crowd that would convene during the proceedings—instead it would be someone completely different. Enter Victoria Redstall.

It is a case that can rival even the greatest of Hollywood classics. Victoria Redstall is the privately educated daughter of one of the top chartered surveyors hailing from Esher, Surrey. She is a well-spoken woman from upper middle class society. Her uncle has been knighted, and one of her cousins married into the Sangster racing dynasty. On the other hand, Wayne Adam Ford is regarded as one of the worst serial killers in the history of California. He murdered four women during his yearlong killing spree, cutting their bodies into tiny pieces afterwards.

One day during his time at the West Valley Detention Center, the former spokes model for breast enhancement supplements walked through the gates of the facility in Rancho Cucamonga, fully determined to speak with him. Victoria has confirmed that she's had a lifelong obsession with serial killers and meeting Wayne in April of 2006, just to interview him for a documentary, was the "dream of a lifetime." She also stated that initially, she was expecting herself to be fascinated with the man, but she wasn't expecting to fall into a deep bond with the man, which ultimately resulted in a disruption in the trial proceedings, and prompted the Sheriff's Department to launch an enquiry. The relationship between the two resulted in a massive furor that spread throughout America.

TV talk shows were unable to figure out what was causing this unlikely friendship to prosper, and why a woman that hailed from such a privileged background would be willing to get in touch with a person who was on trial for four counts of first-degree murder. Prosecutors described him as a "cold blooded monster," yet in an interview with the *Daily Mail*,[viii] then thirty-year-old Victoria Redstall stated, "Wayne is a lovely man. He is funny and charming. Of course, he carried out the most despicable crimes, but am I afraid of him? No. We have sung together in jail and he calls me on a daily basis. We have a wonderful, touching relationship."

In 1994, a few years before Wayne began his killing spree, Victoria Redstall had moved to Los Angeles with hopes of making it big in the world of Hollywood as an actress, even though her only credit was a walk-on role in *EastEnders,* a British soap opera. Since then, she was unable to land any solid roles, working as a bit-part actress mainly. In between her jobs, she stated that she would hang out with police helicopter pilots, and even created a documentary of sorts called "Hover Me: The Making of Helicopter Girl," in which she would stand on her balcony in a nighty while police helicopters would shine the spotlight on her. Redstall first found out about Wayne Ford from a producer friend in 2005, and using her contacts with the police, she was able to get herself within the prison in order to get a meeting with him. Her appearance caused a stir in the courtroom in June, and she was no longer allowed to meet him.

Despite knowing all there is to know about this notorious killer, she has claimed, "From the moment I met Wayne, we bonded. He was shackled and when he was brought in to meet me, he was placed in a wire cage and spoke to me on a phone through Plexiglas. It was like going to see Hannibal Lecter, but I was secretly thrilled. For me, meeting the real life serial killer was a hoot."

For her family, the level of naïveté shown by Victoria was a shock to all who knew her. More importantly, the family was furious that their name was being used in order to justify her actions. Victoria, however, did not show any signs of repentance. She said, "I'm sure some of my family in England will be shocked, but this is a job for me. I adore Wayne. And I'm not some silly little girl. Making a documentary about Wayne was the chance to make a name for myself in Hollywood."

She also revealed to others that for their first few meetings, she used a pseudonym, Clare Smith, which Wayne did not buy. She claimed, "He gave me a Hannibal Lecter stare and said, 'That's not your real name. If I'm going to trust you, you have to be honest with me.'"

Victoria Redstall also provided information regarding their relationship, stating that she would never dress provocatively in order to invoke him in a sexual manner. She said, "I wouldn't dress provocatively when I went to see him. I would always wear a jacket to cover up my breasts.

"He kept begging me to take it off and when I finally did, the only thing he said was, 'You're not that skinny.' He was very interested when I told him I was wearing a padded bra." Victoria was quick to clarify that she does not harbor any loving feelings towards Wayne, despite the deep 'bond' that they share. She says, "We formed a strong emotional bond. But this is a professional relationship. We have never touched. Our letters do not contain anything romantic. People are trying to make out I'm kooky. But I'm just a documentary maker doing her job. This story has taken over my life and I admit being obsessed by him—but not in a sexual way." She also stated that "If Wayne is sentenced to death, it will be a long process of appeals before he finally ends up in the death chamber. But if he wants me there at the end, I will be."

She was given permission by the judge to photograph Wayne, and her obsession came to the point that one of the pictures was used as the background on her cell phone. Ultimately, she was not allowed to take any more pictures within the courtroom. Victoria Redstall also stated that she had lost a number of friends due to her friendship with Wayne. She said that her bond with him was deeply emotional, but not romantic in any way.

"Everyone tells me, 'Be careful, he's a serial killer'… but they don't know Wayne like I do. We've all got evil in us—all of us. He took it to the extent of killing humans…. But I'm going on the man he is today and the remorse that he has today," she says. It is funny, and ironic, that a model for breast enhancement supplements is in a friendship with a serial killer who has a breast fetish, and she does acknowledge this connection. She has referred to it as "hysterical." Clearly the irony is not lost on her. She has also said that she would "trust Wayne with her life."

The case of Wayne Adam Ford is not a unique one, though the timeline (which is very recent) was one that really caused an outbreak of public anger. Victoria Redstall received a lot of attention, and so did Wayne Adam Ford. His trial was concluded on June 27, 2006, where he was found guilty of all four counts of murder. In August of 2006, he was sentenced to death. Currently, he resides on death row at San Quentin State Prison in California. A complicated set of appeals soon followed, with his defense attorney stating his disappointment that the confession and surrender of Wayne himself did not hold more sway within the jury room.

Victoria Redstall was featured on a show called "How to Pick up Girls," which premiered in 2011. Despite the fact that her fledgling career never really attained the heights that she might have dreamed of, her relationship with Wayne Adam Ford was something that really grabbed the headlines and made her an extremely famous person for the better part of six months to a year. As mentioned, her case isn't the only one. There are others, much more properly documented cases that are present, none more so than Theodore Robert Cowell, or as the world might know him, Ted Bundy. Next, we'll follow the story of Ted Bundy, along with the many serial killer groupies that he attracted during his trial.

Wayne Adam Ford

Victoria Redstall

The Handsome, Charming Manipulator... Without a Conscience Ted Bundy

A brutal killer, kidnapper, necrophiliac, and rapist, Ted Bundy was, for reasons clear to all, one of the infamous faces of the 'serial killer era' that gripped the country during the 1960s up until the 1990s. He was born as Theodore Robert Cowell to Louise Cowell on November 24, 1946, at the Elizabeth Lund Home for Unwed Mothers in Burlington, Vermont. Louise Cowell spent eight weeks at the Elizabeth Home before she finally returned to the house of her parents in Philadelphia to raise her new son. For the first few years of his life, Theodore, or Ted, as he was affectionately called at the time, was under the impression that his grandparents were his parents, and that his mother was actually his sister. In 1951, when he was five years old, Ted and his mother moved to Tacoma, Washington, where Louise married Johnnie Bundy, a cook for the military.

Despite the circumstances that he had grown up in, along with the meager resources of the family, Ted Bundy grew up to be an attractive and handsome teenager, who was liked by everybody. He also performed well enough in school. Once high school came to an end, Bundy entered the University of Puget Sound and continued to excel in his academics, but he did begin to suffer a bit of a complex from his peers, who were generally much wealthier than him. Because of the uncomfortable feeling that surrounded him at the University of Puget Sound, Bundy transferred to the University of Washington in order to escape that feeling of financial inadequacy.

In 1966, Bundy opted to study Chinese. One year later, he became engaged to a classmate at the University of Washington, who, in the biographies that were later written about Bundy's life, has been mentioned under a number of different pseudonyms, the most common of which is Stephanie Brooks. Bundy only lasted at the University of Washington for a couple of years, dropping out in 1968, from whereon he began to work a number of a different minimum wage jobs. He also worked as a volunteer at the Seattle office of the presidential campaign that was undertaken by Nelson Rockefeller. In August of the same year, he even attended the 1968 Republican National Convention, which was held in Miami, as a delegate for Rockefeller. Soon after this, however, Stephanie Brooks ended her relationship with Ted Bundy and moved back to her family home in California. She stated her frustration at his perceived lack of ambition, as well as the immaturity that he would often display. Dorothy Lewis, a psychiatrist who reviewed Bundy's case, would later state that this crisis was "probably the pivotal time in his development." Bundy was obviously devastated by what had transpired with Stephanie, and the rejection left him in pieces.

However, he traveled to Colorado, and then moved further east, visiting his relatives in Arkansas and Philadelphia as well, and he even enrolled for a semester at Temple University. It was during this time, in 1969, when Bundy decided that he had to confirm his true parentage, and in order to do so, he visited the office of birth records in Burlington, Vermont.

He returned to Washington in the fall of 1969, where he met Elizabeth Kloepfer. She was a divorcee from Ogden, Utah, who worked as a secretary at the University of Washington School of Medicine. She would become one of the most pivotal figures in his life, and their relationship would continue well past the time he was incarcerated in Utah in 1976. During the early-1970s, Bundy became focused on his life again, and reenrolled at the University of

Washington, this time as a psychology major. He quickly rose through the ranks to become an honor student.

Bundy graduated from the University of Washington in 1972 and joined the election campaign of Governor Daniel J. Evans. He took a series of commitments from thereon, and was finally selected in the law school of UPS and the University of Utah, based upon the recommendation letters that he received from a multitude of different professors under whose tutelage he had studied.

It was during 1973 when Bundy reinitiated his relationship with Stephanie Brooks, while he was still dating Kloepfer. Brooks was impressed at the transformation that he had undergone in the years since they had broken up, and it was evident to her that Bundy was on the cusp of starting a distinguished career in politics and law.

In the fall of 1973, Bundy[ix] matriculated at the UPS Law School, and continued to court Brooks, who even flew to Seattle in order to be with him. They even discussed marriage! Then, in 1974, Bundy abruptly broke off all contact with Brooks; all of the letters that she wrote and the calls that she made were unreturned and unanswered. A month passed without any contact, until one day she got in touch with him via phone. Naturally, Brooks demanded to know why he had just ended the relationship unilaterally without any sort of explanation at all. Biographies state that Bundy replied in a very calm, flat voice, saying, "Stephanie, I have no idea what you mean..." and hung up the phone. She never heard from Ted Bundy again. When he was caught years later and asked about this incident, he replied, "I just wanted to prove to myself that I could have married her."

During this same period, Bundy had begun to skip classes at the UPS Law School. By the start of April, he had stopped going to school completely and women, most of them young, began mysteriously disappearing in the Pacific Northwest.

***

There really isn't any sort of set consensus that depicts when, or precisely from where Bundy began to abduct and kill women. When he was captured, Bundy would tell different stories to different people, and would always refuse to disclose the details relating to the specifics of the earliest crimes that he committed. During the days preceding his execution, Bundy would often provide chilling insights into his murders, accompanied with explicit detail, but he refused to divulge the information of the murders that he committed in the very beginning. He revealed to his defense attorney, Polly Nelson, that he tried to abduct a woman for the first time back in 1969 in Ocean City, New Jersey, though he claimed not to have committed murder until some point in time in 1971, in the city of Seattle.

On the other hand, he told a psychologist by the name of Art Norman that his first killings took place in Atlantic City in 1969, while he was visiting family in Philadelphia. His stories continued to vary, depending upon the person that interviewed him. There are some reports that Bundy might have begun to kill when he was just a teenager. There is substantial circumstantial evidence that suggests in 1961, Bundy, who was fourteen years old at the time, could have kidnapped and murdered eight-year-old Anne Marie Burr, who lived in Tacoma, Washington (the same city where he lived with his mother, Louise). Bundy, however, would repeatedly deny this allegation. The earliest homicides that have been documented usually begin in 1974, when he was twenty-seven years old. According to him, by this time he was extremely proficient and had already mastered the skills that he needed (such as knowledge of DNA profiling) to help him leave as minimal evidence as possible at any crime scene that could be used to incriminate him.

Bundy was a notorious killer—of that, there is no doubt. For instance, on January 4, 1974, soon after he had ended his relationship with Stephanie Brooks, Bundy entered the basement apartment of one Karen Sparks, an eighteen-year-old that is sometimes identified by the names Terri Caldwell or Joni Lenz in his biographies. She was a dancer, as well as a student working at the University of Washington. She was asleep when Bundy entered her apartment. He then bludgeoned her using a metal rod from a bed frame. Then, when she was unconscious, Bundy used a speculum in order to sexually assault her, resulting in a number of horrific internal injuries. Karen Sparks would not regain consciousness until ten days later. However, she did survive, albeit life was never the same for her, as she suffered from permanent brain damage.

Approximately one month after this incident, Bundy broke into the basement residence of Lynda Ann Healy, an undergraduate at the University of Washington.

Lynda was famous for broadcasting morning weather radio reports for skiers in the area. He beat her until she lost consciousness, then dressed her in blue jeans and a white blouse, and even put boots on her feet, before carrying her away.

It was during this period that female college students in the area began disappearing at the rate of about one student per month. On March 12, Donna Gail Manson, a nineteen-year-old student at Evergreen State College located in Olympia (a town sixty miles away, on the southwestern side of Seattle) left to attend a jazz concert, and had only just left her dormitory. Unfortunately, she never arrived at the concert.

On April 17, Susan Elaine Rancourt was headed off to a movie after coming from a meeting of the evening advisors at Central Washington State College, now known as Central Washington University. She never did get to watch that movie. The college is located 110 miles away, on the southeastern side of Seattle. Bundy was establishing a radius, or so it seemed. Women began to come forward, reporting incidents where a man seen carrying a set of books and wearing an arm sling would ask for help in carrying the books to his tan Volkswagen Beetle. Another victim, by the name of Kathleen Parks, vanished after leaving her dormitory at Oregon State University to meet her friends for a cup of coffee at the Student Union building. Again, like in so many cases, she never made it to her destination.

During this time, detectives were becoming more and more worried regarding the disappearances. Detectives from the Seattle Police Department, as well as the King County Sheriff's Department were confused about what was happening. They couldn't find any physical evidence at the scenes, and no pattern could be established between the victims that Bundy was abducting. The only connection was that they were all young, attractive white women. They all parted their hair in the middle. As you can see, it wasn't much to go on at all. There were some reports, however, that a man with brown hair and wearing a sling was the one who was last seen with these women. For instance, when a woman was abducted while walking down a brightly lit alley, heading from her boyfriend's dormitory residence over to her sorority house, she vanished. The next morning, a criminalist, along with several homicide detectives from the Seattle Police Department, combed the whole area, finding nothing at all. This time, reports indicated that people had seen a man on crutches wearing a leg cast in the area, struggling to carry a briefcase. The same tan Volkswagen Beetle was also mentioned.

It was during this period that one of the most popular serial killer groupies entered the picture. While working at the Washington State Emergency Services in Olympia, which was a government-backed agency that was actively involved in searching for women that had gone missing, Bundy met Carol Anne Boone. Boone had been divorced twice and was the mother of two children. Six years later, these two children would play a very important role in dictating the events of Bundy's life.

During this time, six more women were abducted, and the brutal beating of Kathleen Sparks also reached the headlines. As a result, fear amongst women in the area grew significantly and hitchhiking by young women saw a significant drop in numbers. Pressure began to mount on law enforcement agencies to come up with an answer.

It took five more abductions and murders for the King County Police to come up with an accurate description of the man and his car, and subsequently, posters were placed throughout the area of Seattle and adjoining areas. Then aspiring true crime author Ann Rule, as well as

Elizabeth Kloepfer, both saw the sketches as well as the description, and they were sure that the profile fit the frame of the man they knew as Ted Bundy. They even reported him to the police, but with the detectives receiving more than 200 tips on a daily basis, they were in serious doubt that a clean cut student studying law and without any criminal record could be behind such brutal killings.

In August of 1974, Bundy was accepted into the University of Utah Law School, and decided to enroll there, moving to Salt Lake City in the process. At the time, Kloepfer was still in Seattle. Now, as he was studying the first year curriculum for the second time, he began to realize that the other students had some sort of intellectual capacity that he no longer possessed. He was unable to comprehend what was being taught in the classes. Later on, Bundy said, "It was a great disappointment to me."

By August or September of the next year, Bundy had been baptized into the Church of Jesus Christ of Latter-day Saints, even though he often ignored most of the restrictions that the church placed on its members and did not actively participate in the services of the church.

In November, a new series of homicides began to take place, starting with two murders, to which Bundy confessed only a short time before his death. On September 2, he raped and then strangled a hitchhiker in Idaho, who remains unidentified to this day. It was speculated that he threw the body in the nearby river. It is also speculated that he returned the next day in order to photograph, and then mutilate the victim's body.

The next victim to die was sixteen-year-old Nancy Wilcox of Holladay. He raped her, and then thought about releasing her just to "satisfy his pathological urges." However, as he tried to silence her, he ended up strangling her. The body, according to him, was buried near the Capitol Reef National Park, around 200 kilometres to the south of Holladay. It remains unfound to this day.

A number of other deaths also occurred, with the bodies usually being found in an identical manner—nude, with signs of strangulation marks and horrible injuries. More often than not, the bodies were found by travelers or hitchhikers who walked around the roads. One of the deaths was that of a daughter of the police chief of Midvale, another suburb of Salt Lake City. There were numerous other deaths, all of women ranging between the age brackets of fifteen to twenty years old.

In November of the same year, Elizabeth Kloepfer read that women were disappearing in and around Salt Lake City, and decided to inform the King County Police for the second time. Randy Hergesheimer, who was a detective for the Major Crimes Division, conducted a detailed interview with her. By that point, the King County Police had become increasingly suspicious of Ted Bundy, however, when a photo lineup was placed before a Lake Sammamish witness, she failed to identify him.

One month later, Kloepfer called the King County Police again and reiterated her suspicions. The King County Police began counting him in their list of suspects, but there was no credible evidence available that linked him directly to the suspicions. In January of 1975, Bundy took leave after taking his final exams, and returned to Seattle to spend a week with Kloepfer. While there, Kloepfer did not inform him that she had informed the police three times of her suspicions regarding his actions. Instead, she made plans with Bundy to visit him in Salt Lake City in August.

By 1975, Bundy had moved his criminal base from the east side of Colorado to his base situated in Utah. A number of killings took place in that area, again all of those of women who ranged between sixteen to their mid-twenties. Julie Cunningham was twenty-six years old when she disappeared from her apartment as she left for a dinner date with a friend. In later interviews, Bundy informed the investigators of the police force that he had approached her wearing crutches, and had requested her help to carry his ski boots to his car. As they approached the car, Bundy clubbed her, then tied her hands behind her back. He then proceeded to assault her and ultimately strangled her, leaving the body at a remote secondary site situated near Rifle, Colorado, approximately ninety miles to the west of Vail.

Another horrible murder that Bundy committed was that of twelve-year-old Lynette Culver, who was studying at the Alameda Junior High School in Pocatello, Idaho, around 160 miles to the north of Salt Lake City. Bundy lured her out of the school, drowned her, and then sexually assaulted her in a hotel room. The body was ultimately disposed of at a river situated in the northern side of Pocatello.

Around the middle of May in the same year, three colleagues who worked with Bundy in the Washington State Department of Emergency Services visited him. One of them was Carol Anne Boone. They all stayed at his apartment.

Bundy also spent a week with Kloepfer in the early days of June, and even discussed the prospect of marriage the following Christmas. Similar to before, Kloepfer did not mention that she had been discussing his actions with the police behind his back. On his part, Bundy also did not inform her of his relationship with Carol Anne Boone, nor did he tell her of his romantic affiliation with another law student, who is referred to in a number of different accounts as Kim Andrews, or Sharon Auer.

However, Bundy was arrested in 1975 by a police officer of the Utah Police Force when he did not pull over for a routine stop for inspection. The officer noted the following things inside Bundy's car:

- The front passenger seat of his Volkswagen was missing;
- a ski mask was found; along with
- a second mask, made out of pantyhose;
- a crowbar;
- handcuffs;
- a coil of rope;
- an ice pick;
- trash bags; and
- other items that were at the time associated with being burglary tools.

Bundy gave a sufficient explanation for the possession of these items in his car, however Detective Jerry Thompson had a sudden remembrance of a similar suspect from the botched November 1974 kidnapping of Carol DaRonch, and he also remembered Bundy's name from the discussions he had held with Kloepfer over the phone.

Ultimately, as there wasn't a great deal of stuff to incriminate him, Bundy was let go. Later on, Bundy revealed that the searchers had missed out on a collection of Polaroid photographs that he had taken of his victims and hidden in his utility room. He subsequently destroyed those photos.

Bundy was, however, placed on twenty-four-hour surveillance, while Thompson, along with a couple of other detectives, flew to Seattle in order to conduct an interview with Kloepfer. She revealed that she had found objects in his house that did not make any sense to her—a set of crutches; a bag of plaster of Paris (used to make casts, which he later admitted that he had stolen from a supply house); a meat cleaver that had never been used for its original purpose—cooking; surgical disposable gloves; a sack that was full of women's clothing; and an Oriental knife that was kept in his glove compartment. She also revealed that Bundy was usually in debt of everyone he knew, so it was likely that all of the items she had seen had been stolen from one place or another. When she confronted him about the items, Bundy had told her, "If you tell anyone, I will break your fucking neck." She also said that Bundy became terribly upset when she told him that she wanted to cut her hair (like many of his victims, Kloepfer also had long hair, which she parted in the middle). She also revealed that often when she awoke at night, she would sometimes find Bundy under the bed covers, putting her body under scrutiny with the help of a flashlight.

By September, Bundy had sold his Volkswagen Beetle to a teenager from Midvale. Subsequently, the police impounded it, dismantled it, and searched it thoroughly, finding hairs that matched the body of Caryn Campbell, one of his many victims who died a brutal death. On October 2, 1975, Bundy was placed in a lineup before Carol DaRonch, who replied in the affirmative and identified him almost immediately as the man who had tried to kidnap her. While there wasn't enough evidence to link him to Debra Kent, a victim who went missing later that day in the same area, whose body remains missing to this day, there was substantial evidence to charge him with aggravated kidnapping as well as attempted criminal assault in the case of DaRonch. His parents paid his bail of $15,000 and he was freed. He was found guilty of kidnapping and assault, and sentenced to one to fifteen years in the Utah State Prison. While imprisoned, he was found in possession of an 'escape kit,' which contained maps of nearby areas. Later in February of 1976, authorities in Colorado charged him with the murder of Caryn Campbell. He was transferred to Aspen in January 1977.

His first escape took place in Aspen, where he was found after six days by police officers. When Bundy was back in jail at Glenwood Springs, he was told by friends and family to stay put, because the case against him was unlikely to hold up in a court of law. Rather than listening to their advice, Bundy created a more elaborate escape plan. Many visitors helped him obtain the materials required for this plan to work, which included a hacksaw blade, as well as $500 in cash. Carol Anne Boone was a very frequent visitor to the jail, and he later revealed that she had helped him significantly. He escaped on December 30, and his escape from the prison was not discovered until the next day around noon. In the head start that he had achieved, Bundy had already traveled back to Chicago. From there, he moved to Florida.

Sometime during the evening of January 14, or the early hours of January 15, a week after he had fled to Tallahassee, Bundy entered the Chi Omega sorority house of Florida State University, and attacked four women. Twenty-year-old Lisa Levy was asleep in her bed when Bundy beat her unconscious, strangled her, left a deep bite in her left buttocks, sexually assaulted her with a bottle of hair mist, and tore off one of her nipples. In the adjoining bedroom, he turned his attention to Kathy Kleiner, breaking her jaw and lacerating her shoulder deeply before moving on to Karen Chandler. He left her with a crushed finger, a broken jaw, and broken teeth. He then moved to a basement apartment situated eight blocks away, to the residence of FSU student Cheryl Thomas, leaving her with a dislocated shoulder, a broken jaw, and a skull that was fractured in five places. After the attack, she was left with permanent deafness, and also suffered equilibrium damage, which ended her dancing career. On her bed was a stain of semen, along with a makeshift pantyhose mask that included a couple of hairs similar to Bundy's.

On February 12, Bundy knew that the police were closing in on him, and as he did not have enough cash to pay his already overdue rent, he tried to steal a car. Around 1:00 a.m. on February 15, a Pensacola police officer by the name of David Lee stopped him. A routine check revealed that the car was stolen, and when Bundy was told that he was now under arrest, he attacked the officer and began running. The police officer, after firing off a warning shot, gave chase. A scuffle ensued for Lee's gun as he tackled Bundy, but the officer was finally able to subdue him. When the vehicle that he had stolen was searched, an alarming amount of evidence was discovered. There were three different IDs that belonged to female students of Florida State University, a stolen television set, and twenty-one stolen credit cards. As Lee carried Bundy off to jail, he was still unaware that he had just managed to apprehend one of the Top Ten Most Wanted Fugitives on the FBI's list. During the transportation, Lee heard Bundy say, "I wish you had killed me."

He was held for trial in June of 1979. As he had done in his first trial, Bundy handled the defense on his own. Bundy was facing murder charges, with a possible death sentence, and all that mattered to him apparently was that he be in charge of his own case. A pre-trial plea bargain was offered, in which one of the staple terms was that Bundy would be forced to admit to the murders of Bowman, Levy, and Leach, whereas the prosecutors would grant him a sentence of seventy-five years in prison. The prosecutors were positive that this was a deal that could be concluded, mainly because they thought that the "prospects of losing at trial were very good." For Bundy, this was more than just a way to avoid the death penalty, but it was a tactical move. However, right at the last minute, Bundy refused the deal.

The trial was concluded with his conviction for the two murders on July 24, 1979. The death sentence was imposed by the trial judge for the murder convictions. A number of other trials took place, and finally, on February 10, 1980, Bundy was handed the death sentence for the third time, by means of electrocution. It is reported that when the verdict was announced, he stood up and shouted, "Tell the jury that they were wrong!" Nine years later, this would prove to be the death sentence that would ultimately be carried out.

Bundy had a number of love interests, the most notable of which was Carol Anne Boone. While he was on death row, Bundy received more than 200 letters on a daily basis, and he also holds the record for the most number of groupies. During the trial, female groupies literally overran the courthouse with their sheer attendance numbers. The Bundy legend also remains to this day. There existed at the time an old law that allowed legal marriage through a declaration in open court, and taking advantage of this law, Bundy married Carol Anne Boone while his trial was ongoing.

In October of 1982, Carol Anne Boone gave birth to Bundy's daughter, who has for good reason decided not to carry on with her father's surname. It should be known that conjugal visits at the time were not allowed at the Raiford Prison, but the inmates were known to pool money together to bribe the guards to allow them some intimacy with the female visitors. However, the couple's marriage only lasted approximately six years, because in 1986, Boone divorced him, taking her daughter and fleeing the state. When it became clear that the court would not be coming up with any further stays for his execution, Bundy resorted to his last option: he began lobbying, asking his supporters to help him gain executive clemency.

One of his last love interests, a young attorney from Florida by the name of Diana Weiner, even went so far as to ask the families of numerous victims from Utah and Colorado to petition Bob Martinez, the Governor of Florida at the time, to postpone the execution of Bundy, so that he could later reveal more information. However, all of them refused. Martinez clarified that there would be no further delays in the case. To reporters, Martinez said, "We are not going to have the system manipulated. For him to be negotiating for his life over the bodies of victims is despicable."

It is argued by many that Bundy had more admirers when he was on death row than when he was out killing. By the time Bundy had escaped the Glenwood Prison, he had already become a cult figure amongst the women, which made him all the more appealing. He was regarded by many as a "handsome charming manipulator without a conscience." Further adding to his lore was the fact that despite his crazy killing, he was in love with Elizabeth Kloepfer.

While he was on trial in Florida, female followers continued to pour in. His groupie fans ran fan clubs, and widely petitioned to save him from the death penalty. It was incredible at the time to see so many women continuously petitioning for Ted Bundy's clemency, remaining completely oblivious to the fact that he was arguably one of the most horrible murderers to have existed, one who even engaged in necrophilia with the victims he murdered. It goes without saying that the families of the victims must have suffered pain that cannot possibly be translated into words. Even when Bundy began to give gruesome confessions, recounting the details of the murders that he had committed, the obsession of his female groupies did not subside.

Carol Anne Boone continued to provide Bundy with financial assistance even after they were married in the courtroom. Years passed before she awoke to the guilt inside her. It is expected that she now lives under falsified names, with her current whereabouts unknown as yet. Compared to the other women who were completely obsessed with the celebrity status that Bundy had built for himself, Boone was slightly different. For starters, she knew him before he became famous for all the horrific crimes that he had committed. Secondly, Boone was under the impression that Bundy was an innocent man. However, after she left Bundy, for the last three remaining years of his life, Bundy had a constant stream of female followers, including numerous love interests. Even today, there are those who are willing to declare their infatuation with Ted Bundy, making one question how sick minded they might be. I have noticed myself, via several Facebook true crime and serial killer groups, that many women are today infatuated with Bundy. Personally, I think you have to have cold black blood in you to idolize these monsters.

Ted Bundy's account is perhaps one of the most insightful when we consider serial killer groupies. He was a horrific criminal who murdered helpless women in the most gruesome ways possible, and the ones he left to survive were left with permanent injuries that forever altered their lives. The only fault of these women was the fact that they fit the profile of those whom he developed a fetish for, and they suffered terribly for it. Despite the fact that he recalled most of the crimes he had committed, giving numerous interviews to detectives, these serial killer groupies continued to petition for him. It is a sad and damning tale that clarifies the horrific obsession that serial killer groupies suffer from.

Ted Bundy's case brought to light the big issue with serial killer groupies, and the government even began to take certain steps to ensure the obsession that females were developing with serial killers would be toned down. Unfortunately, it did not have the impact that they desired. Numerous fan clubs and groups sprouted, some in universities, others separate altogether, created to celebrate the legacy of Ted Bundy. Females would convene and talk about him long after his death and, as we have already mentioned, there are numerous women out there who will still openly declare how infatuated they are with the actions of this notorious serial killer.

Bob Martinez, the Governor of Florida, knew that if further postponement of the death penalty was afforded to Bundy, it would only cause more problems. Bundy had already become famous on the news throughout the U.S., while other countries had also picked up on his fame and were disseminating news and information about him on television. This was giving rise to more and more groups celebrating Ted Bundy, and ultimately, it was leading to more exposure of this heinous killer. Hence, his death was a much-needed relief for all parties concerned. The families of the victims finally found some peace and solace in the fact that the murderer of their daughters and sisters had been put to justice. It also served as a momentous occasion, highlighting the fact that death by electrocution was still a punishment that the United States could dole out.

Carol Anne Boone, Ted Bundy, and their daughter

The next case that we will discuss is that of Richard Ramirez. Similar to Ted Bundy, Richard Ramirez was another one of the most horrible and heinous serial killers to have existed. He was also similar to Bundy in respect to the fact that he enjoyed the adulation of hundreds of women.

Tell Them It Was the Night Stalker
Richard Ramirez

Ricardo Leyva Munoz Ramirez,[x] also known as 'Richard' Ramirez, was born on February 29, 1960, in the town of El Paso, Texas. Some say that his date of birth was actually February 28. He was the youngest of five children of Julian and Mercedes Ramirez. His father was a Mexican national and a former policeman on the Juarez police force. Later on, he became a laborer on the Santa Fe railroad.

Despite the fact that his father was a hard-working man, he was susceptible to fits of anger, which ultimately led to physical abuse in the household. During his childhood, Ramirez suffered from two major injuries to the head. When he was just a couple of years old, a dresser fell over him, resulting in an injury to the forehead that required thirty stitches. At five, he was knocked out by a swing while playing in the park, and from then on, Ramirez suffered from frequent epileptic seizures that continued until he reached his early teenage years.

At twelve years old, one of the major influences on his life was that of his older cousin, Miguel Ramirez. Miguel was a decorated Green Beret combat veteran of the U.S. Army, and often spoke proudly of some of the horrific exploits that he had carried out during the Vietnam War.

He would also share Polaroid photos that he took of the victims that he'd dismembered, including pictures of the Vietnamese women that he'd raped. For instance, in one photo, Miguel posed with the severed head of a woman whom he'd raped and then killed. Richard, a smoker of marijuana since the age of ten, was deeply fascinated by these stories. Miguel Ramirez was also crucial in teaching some of his military skills to Richard, which he would later misuse to the best of his abilities. These skills included killing with surety and silently. It was also around this period of time when Richard moved out of the house to seek shelter from his father's abuse, instead choosing to sleep in a cemetery located nearby.

Richard Ramirez, known affectionately as Richie in the family, was there to view firsthand as Miguel Ramirez shot his wife Jessie, at point blank range directly in the face with a .38 revolver, in a domestic argument that took place between the couple sometime in May of 1973. After this murder, Richard withdrew himself from other family members, becoming sullen in the process. Soon after, he began to experiment with LSD and he also began to develop an interest in the institute of Satanism. He also learned that his cousin, Miguel Ramirez, whom he had seen shoot his wife, was found to be not guilty by a court of law, by reason of insanity. Miguel was released after serving just four years of incarceration at the Texas State Mental Hospital, in the year 1977. He continued to influence the actions of Richard Ramirez.

As he reached adolescence, Ramirez began to combine his sexual fantasies with acts of violence, such as rape and submissive (forced) bondage. He also began robbing sleeping patrons using a passkey at the Holiday Inn where he worked. One day, as a hotel guest abruptly returned to his room, he saw Richard making an attempt to rape his wife. Richard was beaten out of his senses by the hotel guest and later fired from the hotel.

However, criminal charges were dropped when the couple, who resided in the state of Texas, decided not to return in order to offer testimony against Richard. In the ninth grade, Ramirez dropped out of Jefferson High School. His sleeping habits also became very odd. At age twenty-two, Ramirez moved to California, ultimately settling there on a permanent basis.

The first of his murders was that of a nine-year-old girl by the name of Mei Leung. Her body was found on April 10, 1984, brutally raped, beaten, and then finally stabbed to death. Investigators found her body hanging from a pipe. It took twenty-five years for the police to link Ramirez to the murder via DNA left at the crime scene.

On June 28 of the same year, seventy-nine-year-old Jennie Vincow was also found murdered in her apartment. Her throat had been badly slashed (to the point of decapitation) and she had been repeatedly stabbed while she slept. Numerous other deaths followed. He attempted the murder of twenty-two-year-old Maria Hernandez, who was shot in the face with a .22 caliber handgun. This happened as the poor woman tried to pull into her garage. Inside the house, her roommate, thirty-four-year-old Dayle Okazaki, heard the gunshot and immediately ducked behind the counter as she saw a man enter the kitchen. However, as she raised her head to view whether he was still there or not, Richard Ramirez took one shot, and the bullet became directly lodged in her forehead, instantly killing her.

Less than an hour later, Richard Ramirez killed thirty-year-old Tsai-Lan Yu, pulling her out of her car and effectively killing her with a direct bullet to the head. Note: Although Ramirez is classified as a serial killer, there were times he didn't plan any murders, or have a cooling off period, but instead went on rampage spree killing.

By this point, the media had picked up on the story. Throughout 1985, Richard Ramirez killed countless women, either by invading the privacy of their houses and bludgeoning them to death with items found in their houses, such as hammers, or shooting them in the face. There was no set profile that he followed of the women he murdered. Some were young women, others were old—some of his victims were as old as eighty-three years of age. It should be known that at the time when he began to commit these serial killing murders, Richard Ramirez was a mere twenty-four years old.

On August 24, 1985, Richard Ramirez traveled seventy-six miles in a stolen orange-colored Toyota to Mission Viejo. He broke into the house of thirty-year-old Bill Carns and twenty-nine-year-old Inez Erickson. The couple was asleep at the time when Ramirez entered, and Bill Carns only awoke when he heard the noise of a gun being cocked in the bedroom. Ramirez shot him three times in the head. Then, he turned towards Inez Erickson, first telling her that he was the 'Night Stalker' (the media had begun referring to the mysterious serial killer by this name), and then he forced her to swear that she loved Satan while he bound her hands with neckties that he found in the closet and beat her repeatedly.

He then began searching the household for whatever he could find to steal. Once finished, he dragged poor Inez Erickson to another room, then raped and sodomized her. Sated, he then demanded that Erickson give him more cash and jewelry. Finally, he made Erickson "swear on Satan" that nothing else was left, finally leaving the household. Before leaving, he also told her, "Tell them the Night Stalker was here." As he got back into his Toyota to leave, a thirteen-year-old boy by the name of James Romero III, who lived next door to Bill and Inez, noticed the same guy whom he had spotted earlier in the night, and began to write down the license plate number.

Meanwhile, Erickson managed to untie herself and ventured to the house of a neighbor in order to call for help. Paramedics arrived on the scene, and Bill Carns was rushed to the hospital. The doctors were able to remove a couple of the bullets that were lodged in his head, and he miraculously managed to survive the horrific attack.

As the news broke of the attack, James Romero III told his parents about the "mysterious man in the Toyota," and also provided them with the partial license plate number he had managed to jot down. In turn, they contacted the police. The stolen vehicle was found in Wilshire on August 28, and the police even managed to get a single fingerprint from the rearview mirror, despite the fact that Ramirez had been very careful in making sure that all prints were removed from the car.

An absolute positive match was made, with the fingerprint being confirmed to belong to one Richard Munoz Ramirez,[xi] a twenty-five-year-old drifter who hailed from Texas and who had a significantly long rap sheet, which included numerous arrests for traffic and illegal drug violations. It was decided by officials from the law enforcement agencies to release a mugshot of Richard Ramirez from an arrest that had taken place the previous year, and now the media had finally managed to get a look at the infamous Night Stalker's face.

A subsequent police conference was held, in which the authorities announced: "We know who you are, and soon everyone else will. There is no place that you can hide."

Two days later, on August 30, 1985, Ramirez traveled to Tucson, Arizona, in the hopes of meeting his brother. He was as yet unaware that his face had been shown on the news of every major channel throughout the state of California. When he was unable to meet his brother, Ramirez returned back to Los Angeles on August 31. He easily walked past officers, but as he approached a crowd of people, he noticed that a group of elderly Mexican women were referring to him as "El Matador," which means "The Killer." Confused, he looked around and saw that his face was plastered on virtually every newspaper within the store. In a panic, he began to run, attempting to carjack a woman in the process. However, the bystanders present began chasing him. He jumped over numerous fences, and even tried a couple more carjackings. One of the residents pursuing him threw a metal bar, which hit Ramirez on the head, giving the group the advantage and allowed them to subdue the killer. They held him until police arrived on the scene.

At the very first appearance that he made in court, Ramirez put up a sign of a pentagram, and said, "Hail, Satan." A number of women attended the trial, mostly groupies. Ramirez had a distinctive appeal about his appearance—he was tall, thin, and had a face that most women would find attractive. Despite his heinous crimes, serial killer groupies had become major spectators in the courtroom. Those who attended his trial referred to themselves as "the women in black."

On September 20, 1989, Richard Ramirez was found guilty of all the charges that were levied against him, which included thirteen counts of murder, eleven sexual assaults, five attempted murders, and fourteen burglaries. On November 7, 1989, he was sentenced to death by the gas chamber. The overall cost of the trial was reported to be around $1.8 million, the most expensive in the history of California at the time.

Even before his trial began, there were women who had begun to pay him visits, and were actively writing to him. Starting from 1985, a freelance magazine editor by the name of Doreen Lioy wrote him approximate seventy-five letters while he was incarcerated. She was just one of many, but despite that fact, she remained devoted to him.

At the time, Doreen Lioy was forty-one years old, and she claimed to be a virgin. Logically, because Ramirez also allowed other women to meet with him, Doreen was often disappointed. Doreen sat through every single day of Ramirez's trial, envious of the other women who would also show up without fail, hoping to catch a glimpse or, if luck helped them, the attention of this horrendous man. For them, it was the mere fact that the thrill of danger resulted in sexual arousal. Just the fact that they were in the same room as him was enough.

By 1988, Ramirez had proposed to Lioy and in October of 1996, the two were married at San Quentin Prison in California. Since he was on death row, Doreen Lioy made numerous comments to the public, stating that she would commit suicide if Ramirez was executed. However, like in the case of so many serial killer groupies who get married to serial killers themselves, the two also ended up separating. Because of the lengthy appeals process in California, many people estimated that Ramirez would be somewhere in his seventies by the time he was executed.

While he was awaiting death in prison, Ramirez received countless amounts of mail.

And, according to the revelations made by officials, about ninety percent of those who tried to contact him were women. A spokesman for San Quentin Prison by the name of Lieutenant Sam Robinson once said, "Our high notoriety inmates get the most interest. I have tried to figure this out, but I don't have an answer."

Ramirez didn't marry Lioy because he didn't have a choice; there were a number of women who proposed to him, and before his death, countless women would write letters to maintain regular contact with the notorious serial killer. One of those who wrote to him included a woman from Washington, who was thirty years old at the time. She said that while most of her relatives did not know about her "pen pal from prison," her husband did, and he vehemently disapproved of this act.

This particular woman also made frequent trips to visit him in prison and claimed she started writing to him because she had become so fascinated with his case. She stated that sometimes she wrote him more than twenty letters in a week. She spoke of Ramirez, saying, "He is good looking and I loved his big hands. The thrill of danger of going up to a state penitentiary made it all worth it because to me it was like a dream come true to face one of the world's most feared men." She continued, saying, "Like my mom used to say, you can love someone but you don't have to like them." Perhaps it was relieving to many when she stated that despite being her friend, Ramirez deserved to die for his actions.

When his trial was being held, Cindy Hayden, a member of the jury, also fell in love with him. Cindy had been through a tumultuous childhood. She had grown up with a father who had a terrible temper, while later in life, she herself had been unhappy in her marriage. On February 14, also known as Valentine's Day, she sent Richard Ramirez a cupcake, with the message "I love you" written on it.

This gave Ramirez the impression that she would not convict him. As a result, whenever they were in the same courtroom, he would make it a point to look at her as much as he could. Ultimately, however, it didn't matter—he was not only convicted; he received the worst possible punishment allowed by a court of law. Hayden on the other hand, made a gesture towards Ramirez that she felt remorse for what had transpired.

Ramirez sent an invite for her to meet with him, and she in turn made Ramirez meet her parents. However, despite the devoted efforts of Cindy Hayden, Doreen Lioy ultimately won the battle for Ramirez's twisted heart. And, even though she became Mrs. Richard Ramirez, Doreen stated that she would remain a virgin for life and would never become a mother. Whereas other woman came and went in his life, Doreen remained in her position.

Sheila Isenberg, the author of *Women Who Love Men Who Kill*, in 1991, revealed that she continues to receive messages from women who are charmed by horrific murderers. Some of these women get to meet these killers by virtue of their profession—they are teachers, nurses, or social workers. Others, however, do not get such a chance. Isenberg said, "We Americans romanticize the guy with the gun, whether he's good or bad, their relationships are predicated on the lack of contact. The intensity comes from the fact that the men behind bars have all the time to respond to those letters."

A renowned professor of sociology and criminology at Northeastern University in Boston, Jack Levin,[xii] said that the little amount of scientific research that has been carried out on this phenomenon of serial killer groupies is largely inconclusive. He said that some of these women usually have very low self- esteem, while others enjoy the thrill of being able to come into contact with notorious criminals. Perhaps he phrased it best by saying, "If they had written to a rock star, they would have been lucky if they had gotten so much as a computer-written postcard. Now they even get proposals."

Levin also revealed that some of the women are also intelligent and attractive. The mere fact that these groupies exist, according to Levin, is an insightful detail regarding the inmates themselves. In a large number of cases, he said that the killers are "manipulative, socially screwed psychopaths," who thrive on taking advantage of women who fall for them.

Yet another group of women are driven by charity, rather than being fascinated with these killers. They simply befriend the inmates who are on death row just because they are against the concept of capital punishment, and believe that even those who have been convicted for their heinous crimes should have somebody that they can communicate with. There are even a handful of different organizations that aim to establish 'pen pal' contacts for inmates on death row. A spokeswoman for *Human Writes*, Kay Murphy stated that the organization she works for has 1,300 members, a great number of which tend to write to more than one pen pal in the United States. She clarified that it was a rare occurrence that a romantic relationship would develop between the writer and the inmates. Murphy said, "You have to feel sorry for these people, as it is always going to end in death."

Wedding picture
Ramirez and Lioy

Unfortunately, being a serial killer groupie, especially one who's willing to even marry a serial killer, comes with a certain number of associated risks, as Carol Spadoni later found out. Next, we'll break down the full story of Philip Carl Jablonski.

Want a Pen Pal?
Philip Carl Jablonski

They say that the acorn doesn't fall too far from the tree, and in the case of Philip Carl Jablonski, this holds very true. Jablonski was born on January 3, 1946. It is said that the mind of a child is an extremely easy to mold device. Teach it whatever you want, and the child will learn accordingly. In most cases, he will end up surpassing those whom he learns from. In the case of Jablonski, not only was his view towards life distorted from a very young age, but it turned horrific soon as well. Jablonski was born to a horrible father who beat him, his sisters, and their mother, and even committed murder. His father was an alcoholic, and would frequently sodomize Jablonski's mother, as well as his sisters. If you had a child, you really would not think that such a man would be conducive to the proper upbringing of your child.

Like with many serial killers, most of these guys learn their trade through experience. When he would see his alcoholic father trying to beat his mother, Jablonski would try and protect her.

He was still of a tender age however, and his father would just beat him away with minimal effort. As a result, Jablonski began to suffer from post-traumatic stress disorder, along with numerous other illnesses. At the age of sixteen, this came to the forefront. One day, Jablonski attacked his sister, who was fourteen years old at the time. He put a rope around her neck and threw her onto the bed. He had an erection by that time and told her, "I'm going to get some of that shit off of you." She thought for sure she was going to get raped by her own brother, but suddenly, he just stopped and began to cry uncontrollably.

His sister got up and ran off, and immediately informed their parents. In turn, his father beat him up well and good for his actions.

After leaving high school, he proceeded to join the military and was drafted abroad. Upon his return to the United States in 1968, Jablonski married Alice McGowan. While the two were residing in the State of Texas, Jablonski became sexually violent towards his wife. He would beat her excessively and once, during sex, Jablonski proceeded to put a pillow over her head in an attempt to suffocate her. On a number of occasions, Jablonski strangled the poor girl until she lost consciousness. Despite this violent behavior, he would affectionately call her 'Rose.' He also had a son from her, who, surprisingly enough, is also serving a prison sentence (remember the acorn?).

McGowan eventually began to fear for her life and decided to leave him the same year they married. Subsequently, Jablonski met Jane Sanders in 1968. On their very first date, Jablonski raped her. However, she did not report the rape to authorities. He impregnated her and the two moved to California in July of 1969, when Jablonski decided to take permanent leave from the military. Later, Sanders stated that one time when they were having sex and she wanted to stop, Jablonski pulled out a gun and said, "Don't stop or I'll shoot you!" As she tried to resist, he hit her with the butt of the gun, and she fell unconscious. When she came to a short time later, Jablonski was still penetrating her over and over again. In 1972, Sanders decided that enough was enough, and finally left him.

Even when he was in a relationship with Jane Sanders, Jablonski was not truthful and continued his horrific ways. For instance, in 1970, Jablonski was working as a liquor store clerk, and when a minor entered the store to ask for some alcohol (a common occurrence), rather than refusing the person, Jablonski assaulted the minor sexually. Subsequently, in 1977 and 1978, Jablonski committed several more sex crimes.

In February of 1977, Jablonski met Linda Kimball. Six months later, the couple was living under one roof. In December of 1977, Linda gave birth to their daughter. Time continued to pass without anything happening, until on July 6, 1978, when Linda's mother, Isobel Pahls, felt a nudge on her shoulder as she slept in their home. Turning around, she saw Philip Jablonski towering over her. He told her that he had awakened her so that he could rape her. However, Jablonski did not put his words into action, and when asked why, he told her "all he could see was Linda's face." Pahls was clearly affected, and she immediately rushed out, taking refuge at a neighbor's residence. When Linda found out what had happened, she, along with their daughter, moved out of Jablonski's apartment, and moved in with her mother.

On July 16, 1978, Linda Kimball returned to the residence to collect some items for the baby. Her return to the apartment was the last trip that she would ever make; Jablonski killed her as soon as she entered the threshold of the residence.

An investigation began soon after, and it didn't take investigators a great deal of time to find incriminating evidence against Jablonski. Subsequently, he was arrested and incarcerated for twelve years, finally gaining his release in 1990.

Despite being incarcerated, Jablonski still showed violent behavior. During a seventy-two hour family visit in a prison trailer in 1985, Jablonski assaulted his own mother. Fortunately, his father intervened. Had it not been for his intervention, it is very likely that Jablonski would have ended up killing his own mother as well. Despite the fact both parents survived the attack, the shock and trauma of what had transpired remained with them, and many claim it was one of the factors for their deaths, just six months later.

Like all the serial killers that we have discussed so far, Jablonski also had his fair share of serial killer groupies. Despite the fact that he was overweight, visibly out of shape, and balding, women wanted to be with him. He placed an ad in a newspaper in 1982, which might have been read by numerous people, but one person who was very interested in it was

Carol Spadoni. She began to meet with Jablonski in prison and it wasn't long until the relationship between the two began to turn romantic. It should be stated that while the two were meeting, Jablonski was serving time in the San Quentin Prison for the murder of his previous wife.

Ultimately, the two decided to get married. During his incarceration, Carol and Jablonski would frequently exchange letters with each other. Then, in 1990, Jablonski was released on parole. Before the release, Carol personally visited the parole officer, and requested him not to release Jablonski, saying that she was very scared of her husband, and she certainly did not want him to start living in her house, which she shared with her mother, Eva Peterson. At the time, Carol was forty-six years old, while Eva was seventy-two years old.

Carol's worst fears came to life on April 23, 1991, when Jablonski murdered her and her mother in their house, which was situated in Burlingame. Jablonski started with Carol, shooting her, then suffocating her with duct tape, and finally stabbing her until all life seeped out of her body. He then turned his attention towards Eva, assaulting her sexually and then finally shooting her to death. In a matter of just a few minutes or so, both of the women lost their lives in a horrific and brutal manner.

Their bodies weren't found until three days later. Eva's body was only half-clothed, while her daughter's body had been mutilated; Carol's breast had been sliced open, making visible a silicon implant underneath. It didn't end there, though—and it hadn't started there either.

Fathyma Vann was thirty-eight years old at the time of her death in Indio, California, just one day before Carol and Eva suffered their fates. Vann studied at the same community college that was also attended by Jablonski, a clause that was included as a staple condition for his parole. Fathyma's husband had recently died, leaving her a widow with two teenage girls to care for.

Her body was found lying in a relatively shallow ditch in the desert of Indio. Prior to her death, poor Fathyma had been sexually assaulted, and finally shot. Her eyes had been removed from their sockets, while her ears had also been cut off. It was a horrible death, and investigators were rightly horrified when they saw that the words "I Love Jesus" had also been carved into the victim's back.

Days after the killings of Fathyma, Carol, and Eva, on April 27, fifty-eight-year-old Margie Rogers also lost her life in Grand County, Utah. Jablonski was en route to kill two of his pen pals who wrote to him in prison—one who resided in Kentucky, and the other in Tennessee. Fortunately, however, this just could not materialize.

Jablonski was not a killer with a lot of finesse. When a Kansas Highway Patrol Officer stopped him on the road, a routine search of the car provided the law enforcement agency with enough evidence to convict him. A tape recorder was found, which Jablonski had used in order to recall all of the crimes that he had committed, in chilling detail, along with the names of the victims and the means with which he had killed them. Then, there was a belt, made out of the skin of a snake, which included all of the names of the women that he had already killed, and those whom he planned to kill. In total, Jablonski had murdered five women. He was captured for good this time.

He was arrested and convicted of first-degree murder for each of the five women. In 1996, he was placed in San Quentin Prison, along with numerous other serial killers on death row for horrific murders.

Jablonski claims to be an artist, and he is into crafts, creating numerous different things that can be purchased by others. From then on to this day, Jablonski has remained at San Quentin Prison. Similar to the time that he served before for the murder of Melinda Kimball, Jablonski has placed numerous ads in a number of websites in different countries, looking for female or male pen pals who would write to him frequently.

On one German website, Jablonski claims himself to be a "gentle giant," and his description of himself includes terms such as "very understanding and loving." Here's an (unedited) ad that he placed on a website:

I ask your indulgence male and female and promise to be brief as possible, allow me to introduce myself as Death Row Teddy.
I am 58 years old. My DOB is January 3rd 1946.
I have been on death row for 11 years. (Aug.1994)
I am seeking for a female/male Teddy Bear.
I lost once my heart scarcely used by one careless owner.
As I saw it last it was thubbing in your direction.

Caucasian male - seeking an open minded male/female for unconditional correspondence on mature and honest level, that has a caring heart to create a special friendship build from the heart.

Why choose me?

I am a professional artist, photography, amateur poet, writer, masseur, college educated, not a rude person, like to party, travel. My home town is Joshua Tree, CA. I am very understanding and loving. I believe in giving a second chance. People describe me as a gentle giant.

I love cats, dogs, parrots, horses and teddy bears.

What I like in a friend? I like it if you like to travel, party. Someone who is mature and wants a honest friendship. Someone who is able to discuss personal issues on a mature level and is not scared of Frank discussion.

What I miss the most: Traveling, photography male and female company, giving massages, partying, walking in the rain, romantic walks on the beach, romantic candle light dinners, cuddling in front of a roaring fire, soft music.

Lets share our thoughts and feelings (good or bad) lets learn about one another freely and

watch our friendship bloom like a rose and be strong as a castle wall which can't be broken.
A loving heart is worse more then a mountain of gold.
Love communicates on any subject or issue. Write me please you won't be disappointed.
Don't let my situation stop you from writing me. Pick up your pen and pay me a visit.
Guaranteed response.
Sincerely,
Phillip

If you care to write, this is his address:

Phillip Carl Jablonski
Prison Inmate C-02477
San Quentin State Prison
San Quentin, CA 94974
USA

***

Carol Spadoni was fooled by one of such ads back in 1982, and ended up losing her life. It took her less than a year to decide that she wanted to marry this man. While many serial killer groupies are usually obsessed by such heinous men, only a handful decide that they would want to marry these men. Most women who write to serial killers only claim to do so because of the thrill of writing to somebody who has killed in a brutal fashion.

It is all good and fine when they are meeting this caged animal that lives behind bars. But when they are released, things can go awry, as they do in most cases. Carol Spadoni was an avid visitor while Jablonski was in prison, while she was also a frequent writer to him. However, as we mentioned, she already knew how violent this man could be, and was slowly trying to cut all contact and move away from him. The parole officer, to whom she requested that Jablonski should not be released, paid little heed to her words, and ultimately, she paid the price for her affiliation with this murderer.

At the time of this writing, Jablonski is sixty-eight years old, and often writes to pen pals stating his lack of remorse about killing those women, as well as the regret that he harbors inside for not killing his mother when he had the chance. Despite the fact that he killed only five women (a small number, compared to the other horrible murderers that we have discussed in this book), all of the murders were committed in a similar fashion, hence befitting the profile of a serial killer.

The lives and deaths of Carol Spadoni and her mother Eva Peterson serve as stark reminders that women should not become so strongly affiliated with these serial killers, as they can often come back to haunt that person for the rest of their lives.

Unfortunately, in the case of Carol Spadoni, it didn't pan out so well. While she wrote and often gave interviews to the media about how Jablonski was a misunderstood man and how he had changed, the fact that Jablonski ended up killing five women in quick succession just goes to show that it is very difficult for such men to really bring about a change. Most serial killers become sexually aroused by the act of killing.

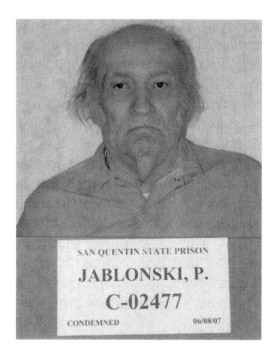

Phillip Carl Jablonski - 2010

Almost all of the cases we have covered thus far are those in which the killer either sexually assaulted the body of the woman whom they attacked, or caused harmful physical injury to her, either before or after killing her. The next case that we shall talk about is a particularly disturbing one, primarily because the criminal's trial is still ongoing, and secondly because of the avid tries made by the criminal himself to prove that he is 'mentally unstable' in order to avoid justice. Remarkably though, despite the despicable acts that have been committed by this individual, there are numerous women who support him and actively lobby for his vindication.

This is the story of Luka Magnotta, and a crime that is borne straight out of the most horrific nightmare you could ever imagine.

Attention Seeker
Luka Magnotta

Luka Rocco Magnotta (born as Eric Clinton Kirk Newman) was born on July 24, 1982, in Scarborough, Ontario, Canada. He went to school at the I. E. Weldon Secondary School, situated in Lindsay. When he was a teenager, Eric Newman was diagnosed with borderline schizophrenia. In 2003, at the age of twenty-one, he started to appear in pornographic videos made solely for the gay community, often working as a male escort and a stripper too.

In the 2005 issue of *FAB* magazine,[xiii] which circulates around Toronto, Magnotta appeared as a pin-up model under the pseudonym 'Jimmy.' He also competed in the reality series called "COVERguy," which is broadcast on OUTtv. He also began undergoing numerous plastic surgeries, and then made an appearance in a Slice Network show called "Plastic Makes Perfect," back in February of 2008.

It seems a stable enough life for a man that should be named in this book. However, his run-ins with law enforcement agencies began around the time he was twenty-three years of age.

117

This 22-year-old soccer fan was born in Russia and currently lives in Toronto. He hopes to train to become a police officer. "I don't want to do traffic tickets. I am thinking vice or homicide." Jimmy likes men and women in uniforms. He says his best attribute is "my package. I got a mean dick. Me and my buddies made a few videos." Jimmy has also been a model for Sears, sporting "pyjamas, jeans, sweaters." When it comes to pizza, he prefers "Greek style with feta cheese and black juicy olives."

His email is stunningstud21@hotmail.com.

In 2005, Magnotta was convicted of one count of impersonation, along with three counts of fraud, after he impersonated a woman in order to apply for a credit card so he could purchase goods that had a value in excess of $10,000. Upon pleading guilty, he was sentenced to a conditional sentence of nine months, along with a probation period of twelve months.

Eric Newman legally changed his name to Luka Magnotta on August 12, 2006. In March of 2007, Magnotta declared bankruptcy, with the total outstanding amount owed against him being around $17,000. By December of the same year, his bankruptcy was fully discharged. In the same year, numerous rumors began to emerge that Magnotta was romantically involved with Karla Homolka, a triple killer from Canada with a very high profile.

However, in a subsequent interview that he gave to the *Toronto Sun*, Magnotta clearly denied having any such relationship. It was found later on during his murder investigation that this was a lie.

A huge number of profiles were created on numerous different social media websites, as well as discussion forums, mainly to falsify different claims or plant rumors regarding

Magnotta. This gave Magnotta the option to repeatedly hit the news, as he would vehemently deny such allegations and claims against him, blaming 'cyber stalking.' As per the information that was released by the police, it was found that Magnotta had created a minimum of seventy Facebook pages himself, and also set up twenty different websites under separate domain names.

However, thus far, what you have read about Magnotta is pretty much the story of a struggling actor who craved attention. Reading this information is unlikely to provide any sort of hint regarding the heinous crime that he committed. Unfortunately, his actions forever ended the life of one Lin Jun, while the police continue to find out articles of evidence that link Magnotta with murders of other people.

***

Lin Jun was born on December 30, 1978, and was commonly known as Justin Lin to his friends. He was an international student who hailed from Wuhan, and was an undergraduate in the facility of engineering and computer science at Concordia University. To support himself, Lin was also working part time as a clerk for a convenience store, which is situated in Pointe-Saint-Charles, Montreal. On May 1, 2012, Lin had moved into an apartment situated in the Griffintown area, along with a roommate. His friends last reported seeing him on May 24, and also reported getting a text message from him at around 9:00 p.m. that night.

Justin Lin was a dedicated student, punctual to work, managed his time well, and wouldn't miss work without informing his boss beforehand. When he did not show up for work the next day, his boss therefore, became suspicious. Three of his friends decided to visit his apartment on May 27, and when they couldn't find him there, they pondered upon where he must have gone. He was reported to the police as missing on May 29.

R.I.P. Lin Jun

Unbeknownst to them at the time, on May 25, a video with a running time of eleven minutes, and entitled "1 Lunatic 1 Ice Pick," was uploaded to a website called bestgore.com. The video showed a naked male, tied to the frame of a bed, while being stabbed over and over again with an ice pick, as well as a kitchen knife, after which he was dismembered. The last thing the video showed were acts of necrophilia being carried out. The perpetrator who made the video, made use of a fork and a knife in order to cut off part of the victim's flesh, and then called in a dog to chew on the body. In the background, a 1987 song by New Order, called "True Faith," could be heard playing. On the wall, a 1942 poster of the hit film *Casablanca* was visible. This immediately raised the attention of the Canadian authorities, and they were soon able to acquire a more extensive version of the video, which gave them enough information to confirm that cannibalism might also have been performed.

On the internet, material that was already promoting the video was made available approximately ten days before the murder even took place. On May 26, an attorney from the city of Montana called up the Toronto Police and reported the video, while simultaneously also informing the Federal Bureau of Investigation and the local sheriff. The officials, perhaps not so surprisingly, dismissed the report. Viewers of the website bestgore.com also tried to report the video. It wasn't until later that the police confirmed the authentication of the video.

On May 29, 2012, at approximately 11:00 a.m., a package was received at the national headquarters of the Conservative Party of Canada. When opened, it contained a man's left foot. There was already a foul smell coming from the package, and it had been stained with blood. A 'red heart' symbol had also been marked on it.

Upon inspection of the package that was delivered to the headquarters of the Conservative Party, a note was found, stating that a total of six body parts had been mailed to different addresses, and that there would be another killing. Three other packages that had already been recovered also contained notes, though the police decided against revealing their contents, because they feared copycats might make it difficult to locate the killer.

The Canada Post processing facility then found another package, intercepting it midway;

the intended recipient of this package was the Liberal Party.

A janitor, who worked daily to collect the trash from a garbage pile in an alley situated behind an apartment building in the Snowdon area in Montreal, had first seen a suitcase in the trash on May 25. However, due to his excessive workload that week, he was unable to pick it up. When he did open it up to view the contents, to his horror, he found a decomposing torso inside. Without hesitation, he called in the authorities.

The police conducted a thorough search of the area, and found numerous remains of the human body, along with clothes that had been bloodied, papers that provided an identification of the subject, as well as a number of "sharp and blunt objects" from the back of the alley. When surveillance camera footage was reviewed, police saw a suspect lugging a number of different garbage bags outside, and the image of the suspect was very similar to the one captured at the surveillance video of the post office in Côte-des-Neiges, where the packages containing body parts had been mailed.

Soon after, police searched apartment 208, where Luka Rocco Magnotta officially resided (on a rental). He had been living there for four months, and his rent had been paid up to June 1. Before he had left the apartment, most of the items from the apartment had been moved out. However, the police found blood on the mattress, the bathtub, a table, as well as the refrigerator. On the inside of the closet, written in red ink, were the words: "If you don't like the reflection. Don't look in the mirror. I don't care."

On May 30, 2012, the police were able to provide confirmation that the body parts all belonged to one man: Lin Jun. The police were also quick to identify Magnotta as the primary suspect, who had fled by that time.

On June 5, 2012, a package was delivered to St. George's School, while another package at False Creek Elementary School in Vancouver was handed over to authorities. The package sent to St. George's School contained a right foot, while the package sent to False Creek Elementary contained a right hand. Both the schools were shut down immediately and reopened the next morning. Investigations revealed that the packages had been delivered from Montreal.

DNA samples were retrieved from the family of Lin Jun, and the four limbs, as well as the torso, were matched together. However, his head was still missing. It wasn't until the police received an anonymous tip on July 1 when his head was found near the corner of a small lake situated within Angrignon Park in Montreal.

On July 11, Lin Jun's body was cremated, and his ashes were put to rest on July 26, 2012 at the Notre-Dame-des-Neiges Cemetery in Montreal.

The Service de police de la Ville de Montreal (SPVM) issued an arrest warrant for Luka Magnotta, which was subsequently upgraded to a Canada-wide warrant by the Royal Canadian Mounted Police.

Luka Magnotta was accused of committing the following crimes:

- First-degree murder;
- Committing an indignity to a dead body;
- Publishing obscene material;
- Mailing obscene, immoral, indecent or scurrilous material; and
- Criminally harassing Canadian Prime Minister along with several other members of Parliament.

At the behest of the Canadian authorities, Interpol put forth a Red Notice on May 31, 2012, and for a number of days before, as well as after, his arrest, Magnotta's photos were put on display right at the top of the official homepage of the Interpol website. The request made by the Red Notice was that Magnotta be provisionally arrested "pending extradition back to Canada by any member state of Interpol."

Using a false passport under the name of Kirk Trammel, Magnotta had taken a flight from Montreal to Paris on May 26. Police were able to track the signals emanating from his cell phone to a hotel situated in Bagnolet, but by the time they arrived on the scene, Magnotta was gone. The hotel room contained pornographic magazines. Magnotta had contacts in Paris following a trip he had taken earlier back in 2010. From Paris, Magnotta boarded a Eurolines bus from the Bagnolet coach station, which was headed to Berlin, Germany.

On June 4, 2012, however, the manhunt came to an end, when Berlin Police apprehended Magnotta at an internet café, where he was sitting reading the news that had spread about himself. At first, he tried to defend himself, giving police fake names. However, he ultimately relented and revealed his true identity.

Fingerprint evidence was enough to remove all doubts of his true identity. On June 5, 2012,

Magnotta made an appearance in a court in Berlin. As per the information released by German officials, Magnotta did not oppose extradition. There was significant evidence already available to keep him in custody until extradition could be carried out, and Magnotta himself relented to a simplified procedure.

Magnotta was extradited back to Canada and landed at the Mirabel International Airport, from where he was placed in solitary confinement at the Rivière-des-Prairies Detention Center.

By this time, Magnotta was well known throughout Canada. He was named as the 'Canadian Newsmaker of the Year'[xiv] by the media, resulting in great controversy. Importantly, Lin Jun's family also arrived at the Trudeau Airport in Montreal. Chinese students had set up a fund to pay the family's expenses while they stayed in Canada, while a candlelight vigil was also held in city. On June 19, Magnotta made an appearance in court via video satellite, pleading not guilty through his lawyer. Two days later, he appeared in person at a high security courtroom to request a trial by jury.

The evidence that was showcased was subject to a publication ban, though it is reported that a number of horrific items were shown, including the video itself, as well as photographs of the remains of the victim. Magnotta, along with Lin's father, both fainted numerous times during the proceedings.

As it often is with court cases, it was another ten months before Magnotta was actually indicted. On April 12, 2013, Luca Rocco Magnotta was indicted on counts of first-degree murder, offering indignities to a dead body, distribution of obscene materials, employing the postal service to distribute obscene materials, as well as criminal harassment. By this time, numerous support groups were also created on social media to voice the support for Luka Magnotta.

On September 29, 2014, the opening statement was made of his trial, which was expected to last for a total of six weeks. The jurors were instructed that Magnotta "admits the acts or the conducts underlying the crime for which he is charged. Your task will be to determine whether he committed the five offences with the required state of mind for each offence."

One of the Facebook pages, run by administrator Tiffiee Da KittyLady, says, "We may not be **fans** of what he did, but I believe in him as a person, and loved him before all this happened... L." The page has sixty members so far. Another group, also set up on Facebook, by one Allyssa Kerr, is "for people who are fastiated [sic] with Luka, or anything that goes against society, and their morals, or who would just want to have sex with him." The group has approximately 170 members. It should also be noted that these groups are mostly populated by young women.

Some have even said that they find the video, in which Magnotta kills, dismembers and then eats the flesh of Jun's body, to be "inspirational." What could be inspiring about such a video is anybody's guess. Another group, entitled "Support Luka Magnotta" and run by Destiney St. Denis, a twenty-one-year-old from Saskatoon said in an email revealed by the *National Post*, "I like Luka Magnotta because he is inspirational, nice, and very, very good looking. I have seen the video over 20 times. I do think that was him, and I liked it. He is inspirational because he is not afraid of himself."

Perhaps not so shockingly enough, St. Denis also said that she has no regard for the feelings of Lin Jun's family. "I think that if anyone is a victim in this case, it is Luka... because of all the bullying that he had to endure prior to the murder," she writes. "I've seen worse in horror films. I really like horror films. He's a very nice person. We talked a lot about fashion design."

Another supporter, who goes by the name Lexa Mancini, and is the administrator of a blog called "Luka Magnotta Obsession," did admit, however, that her interest in him was a hard thing to understand. "I'm aware that there is some cognitive dissonance involved in supporting Luka the way I do," she wrote. "It's just impossible to reconcile the beauty and the beast within him. On the one hand, I adore this image he has created for himself, even though I'm fully aware it's not real. As has been pointed out, his surgically altered face is not even real, but this just doesn't make him any less attractive."

Furthermore, Luka Magnotta is also allegedly the person behind a number of videos that showcase animal cruelty, specifically those that involve the killing of cats. In one video, which was uploaded to YouTube back in 2010, entitled "1 boy 2 kittens," a man can be seen suffocating two kittens using a vacuum cleaner. A number of other such videos exist. Another person, by the name of Anne Leroy, a member of the group "Luka Magnotta is Awesome!!!"

131

wrote (unedited), "Generally , for the Valentine day, lot of beautiful cards can be found, also , as last year , I propose you to buy one for Luka . Of course, he is not our lover , just we support him, but a beautiful card with tenderness can give him warm in his heart...and that is the most important..."

She also wrote the following unedited passage: "I hate reporters more and more , all have made it a pleasure to denounce with ironic term the excess weight of Luka ... as if some morality played in that sense... they were very upset to contemplate a young man of great beauty in front of that crime ... What worries me is his health, as from June 2012 to March 2013 it took a bit of weight ... that is normal , lack of activity , probably two meals a day , no sport .....while the last week of freedom for him had been extremely stressful ... it's normal ... on other side, he took a lot of weight between April and November , only in six months proves that the treatment does not suit him , if he has a weak voice proves he is sick , too many drugs and is unkempt , with no one to worry about ... what they want? to kill him slowly ?

"What does his lawyer do to ensure that his client is in good health, that drugs are suitable for him or can be reduced if needed and he can receive sufficient exercise to be in shape and be himself with dignity. In addition, the Court send a man to the Court in comatose state....Is it ethics to do that ??? ..How he will be able to defend himself at the trial ??"

These are statements written by everyday users on social media, depicting their interest in Luka Magnotta, as well as what he means to them. While most of the women who write such statements openly acknowledge that they know that Magnotta has had a number of artificial surgeries and isn't exactly 'true,' they are just drawn into his good looks. The fact that he is also famous, and considered by many as a victim, further adds to his overall appeal. Despite the horrific acts that he has committed, Luka Magnotta continues to drum up support on social media, and the trial continues, with the sole purpose of determining whether Luka Magnotta was sane or not, as he has already admitted to committing those murders.

The next case that we shall discuss is that of a true crime author and serial groupie who has been affiliated with a number of serial killers. Her name is Sondra London, and her story spans the next two chapters, as she was associated with two different serial killers, Gerard John Schaefer and Danny Rolling.

Gerard John Schaefer was born on March 25, 1946. He was the first of three children, born to Gerard and Doris Schaefer, both of whom were Catholics. Despite being born in Wisconsin, Gerard was raised in the city of Atlanta, Georgia, where he studied at Marist Academy until the year 1960. From there, Gerard and his family moved to Fort Lauderdale, Florida. There, the Schaefers joined numerous yachting and sailing clubs.

From a very early age, Gerard was unable to bond well with his father. His father was a drunkard and a womanizer. With the passage of time, the two continued to grow apart. Gerard was of the belief that both of his parents usually favored his sister over him, later claiming that he was the "illegitimate product of a forced marriage." As he entered his teenage years and hit puberty, Gerard became obsessed with women's panties (he would collect them), and he also became a 'peeping Tom,' as he began to spy on a girl who was his neighbor, by the name of Leigh Hainline. Schaefer had also begun to steal women's underwear, and often had long fantasies about dying. Furthermore, he would

135

also tie himself to trees, just because it aroused him sexually.

Later on, Gerard admitted that he killed animals when he was a young man, and would also indulge in cross-dressing (wearing women's clothing). At times, he has claimed that he only cross-dressed in order to avoid getting drafted for the Vietnam War—and, in fact, he did manage to avoid it. He also hunted animals that could not be consumed, often in the Everglades. He also met his first girlfriend, Cindy, around this time, and despite their unorthodox sex life, they remained in a relationship for three years. Schaefer would often make her participate in 'role play' situations, where they would act out his fantasies, tearing off her clothes and then pretending to 'rape' her. In 1963, however, Cindy broke up with him.

Upon his graduation from St. Thomas Aquinas High School in 1964, Schaefer enrolled in college for an associate degree in business administration, which he managed to complete. He also tied the knot around this time.

In 1968, he applied for a teacher's license at the Florida Atlantic University, which he was subsequently granted. A year later, Schaefer became a teacher. Unfortunately, his tenure as a teacher at Plantation High School was short lived, as he was soon fired by the principal for the exhibition of what was described as "totally inappropriate behavior." Schaefer then tried to move towards priesthood, only to be turned down.

By 1968, Schaefer's wife had filed for divorce, citing "excessive cruelty" as the primary reason. He began working as a patrolman during this time and met Teresa Dean one night as he patrolled the area in his security guard uniform. The two had hit it off, and married soon after. From there, Schaefer decided to opt for law enforcement as a career choice, and in 1971, at the age of twenty-five, Gerard John Schaefer was able to secure a job as a police man, even though he had failed the psychological test when he put through his application.

Yet again, his job tenure was short lived, as he was fired. This time, Schaefer had been using the personal information of female traffic offenders in order to ask them out on dates. From there on, he moved to Martin County, where he got another job in law enforcement, though this time he was promoted up to Deputy Sheriff. It was during this time when Schaefer first started displaying deadly behavior towards women.

One day, Pamela Sue Wells and Nancy Ellen Trotter, aged eighteen and seventeen, were looking to hitchhike a ride in Stuart, Florida. On that same road, Deputy Sheriff Gerard Schaefer was traveling in his police cruiser when he stopped alongside the two. Upon getting out, he took their details, and told them that hitchhiking was illegal in Martin County, which was a lie. The girls were staying at a halfway house, and Schaefer agreed to drive them back. Upon dropping them off, Schaefer offered the two girls a ride to the beach the following morning. This was an officer of the law; there was absolutely no reason for Wells and Trotter to doubt his integrity, or his words, for that matter. So, they happily accepted. The next morning, the Deputy Sheriff kept his commitment, and was on time to pick the two girls up.

However, rather than taking the girls to Jensen Beach as promised, he drove them to the swampy Hutchinson Island, located off State Road A1A. When the girls asked what he was doing, Schaefer, then twenty-six years old, said that he wanted to show the girls an old Spanish fort. Upon reaching the location, Schaefer began making sexual remarks, finally pulling out a gun and telling the two girls that he had planned to sell them off as "white slaves" to a foreign prostitution syndicate. He handcuffed the girls and then placed a gag in both of their mouths. Dragging them out of the car, he left them balanced on the roots of a tree, with nooses tied around both of their necks. Had they slipped and fell, the girls were likely to have broken their necks and died.

It was at this moment when his police radio began to buzz. Answering the call, Schaefer promised that he would return for the girls before he drove away. When he left, the girls frantically began to untie themselves, and finally succeeded. They then proceeded to the nearest police station, which was ironically the same police station where Schaefer used to work.

Soon after, Schaefer returned back to the woods, only to find the loose bonds and both of the girls gone. Realizing that he was in hot water now, he called back to the station, and while speaking to the Sheriff Richard Crowder, he claimed, "I've done something foolish. You're going to be mad at me."

In order to supplement his explanation, he said that he had pretended to kidnap and then threaten to kill the two strangers whom he met hitchhiking on the road, so that they would be scared in the future of using "such an irresponsible method of traveling." Logically, Schaefer's boss did not believe his explanation, and called Schaefer over to the station.

Upon his return to the headquarters, Sheriff Richard Crowder fired Schaefer on the spot, and had him arrested. He was charged with false imprisonment, as well as two counts of aggravated assault. However, Schaefer made his bail of $15,000 and was released on July 24, 1972. Since he had no defense at all against the charges levied at him, he cut a plea bargain in November of the same year, and then pleaded guilty to one count of aggravated assault, while all other counts were dismissed against him.

When his sentencing was held three days before Christmas, the presiding judge, D. C. Smith, said that Schaefer was "a perfect jackass" and a "thoughtless fool." He was then sentenced to one year in jail, as well as three years of probation. However, it was stated that if he kept up good behavior within prison, he would gain release within six months. This meant that by June, he would be out on the roads and on the prowl again.

Throughout the time that he was in prison, Schaefer would pass his time by writing stories. His cell mate, whose name was Emmerson Floyd, later recalled that Schaefer would not allow anybody to read whatever he had written, but would often enjoy reading his stories aloud. Most of the stories, as Floyd revealed, were brutal in nature, and included some horrible things that he considered to be "hair-raising."

Only a couple of months after the assault on Trotter and Wells, on September 27, 1972, while Schaefer was out on bail, two more girls, seventeen-year-old Susan Place and sixteen-year-old Georgia Jessup had vanished from Fort Lauderdale. Place's parents revealed that the two girls were last seen leaving with an elderly man, who claimed that his name was Jerry Shepherd, and that they were going to a nearby beach where they could play the guitar. Sadly, it was their last trip.

However, Susan's mother had a suspicion that something wasn't right, and as such she had managed to write down the license plate number of the Datsun that 'Jerry Shepherd' had driven. Unfortunately, she made a slight error in copying the tag's prefix, writing down 4, which was Pinella County, rather than 42, which represented Martin County. Half a year passed before Susan's mother realized her error. However, when she did rectify it, the trace led her to Schaefer.

On March 25, 1973, Susan Place's mother arrived at the Martin County Jail, where Schaefer was serving his one-year sentence, with a picture of her daughter in her pocket. Schaefer categorically denied to have ever laid eyes on the girl.

On April 1 of the same year, hikers traveling near Blind Creek on Hutchinson Island found human bones. As soon as he heard the news, Schaefer began to tear up the short stories that he had written, and throw away the pieces. With the help of their dental records, the two teenage girls were identified. Susan Place had been shot straight in the jaw from close range. According to the specifics of the crime scene, it was revealed that the two girls had been tied to a tree and brutally butchered.

Based upon the testimony given by Lucille Place, as well as the *modus operandi* (the killings bore a stark resemblance to the way in which the Trotter-Wells case had panned out), the police only had one suspect in mind: Gerard Schaefer.

His mother's home was subsequently searched on April 7, and some of the objects that were seized in the raid included a purse, whose ownership belonged to Susan Place, three articles of jewelry that reportedly belonged to twenty-five-year-old Leigh Bonadies, who had been reported missing in September of 1969. Other items included a couple of teeth, as well as a shamrock pin that belonged to twenty-two-year-old Carmen Hallock, who had been reported missing in December of 1969.

There were also news clippings within the apartment that divulged details regarding the Hallock, as well as the Bonadies case, an address book that originally belonged to twenty-two-year-old Belinda Hutchens, who had been missing since January 1972, as well as a diary, a passport, and a poetry book that belonged to one Collette Goodenough, who was last spotted in January of 1973. There was also a driver's license that belonged to nineteen-year-old Barbara Wilcox, whose disappearance occurred simultaneously along with Goodenough. The police also recovered an article of jewelry that originally belonged to a fourteen-year-old girl by the name of Mary Briscolina, who had gone missing, along with a female friend, in October 1972, an envelope with the recipient being Jerry Shepherd, thirteen knives as well as eleven guns, along with hundreds of photos of women yet unknown to the police, along with pictures of Schaefer himself clad in female underwear.

There were more than 100 different writings and stories that were also present within the house, all of which detailed the murder and the horrific torture of prostitutes.

Funnily enough, Gerard Schaefer had an explanation for everything, despite the fact that the evidence was explicitly incriminating. He stated that all of the weapons were legal, with some of them being souvenirs from the war. He said that Lucille Place was mistaken regarding the purse that she believed belonged to her daughter; he said that he had bought it on a trip to Morocco back in 1970. He stated that he had retrieved the Wilcox-Goodenough documents while he was on patrol and, guessing they might be useful, he had kept them. Then, he stated that Leigh Bonadies, one of his neighbors in the past, had given him jewelry as a gift. He stated that the stories were just transcriptions from a psychiatrist, from whom he received treatment back in 1968. He claimed that the psychiatrist had told him to write down "whatever crossed his mind."

When interviewed about the teeth, he stated that they must have been planted by his current roommate (police did interview the roommate and let him go).

Prosecutor Robert Stone heard all of the explanations given by Schaefer, yet bought none of them. Subsequently, he was charged with two counts of murder and held on a bond of $200,000. Schaefer claimed, "I'm sick and I hope to God you can help me."

On September 17, 1973, his trial got underway. The two teenagers who had once escaped, Nancy Trotter and Pamela Wells, both made an appearance to testify against him, telling the court of his affiliation with tying girls to trees. Lucille Place also did her part, telling of how he had left with her daughter, as well as Georgia Jessup. On the other hand, three witnesses who acted as an alibi for Schaefer claimed that he was sick in bed, but their testimony was disregarded, and he was convicted on September 27, 1973.

Schaefer filed nineteen appeals while in jail, whereas his wife, Teresa Schaefer, made just one visit in order to serve him with divorce papers. In 1987, a judge who had become tired of all the appeals said, "The defendant should realize, once and for all, that the die is cast, the mold is made, the loaf is baked. Therefore, the judgment is final and forever."[xv]

***

Usually, the serial killer groupies that are attracted by such men usually come to the forefront when the men are in jail, or when their trial is ongoing.

In Schaefer's case, it was when he entered jail. In 1979, Schaefer claimed that he had married a "picture bride" from the Philippines. The woman made her first appearance in July of 1980, when she moved in with Schaefer's father. A marriage license was also shown, and subsequently accepted by the Avon Parks maximum-security prison. A number of contact visits were allowed by the prison, but as it turned out, the woman was only using Schaefer to get a green card, which she did in 1985. When she did, she subsequently divorced the convicted killer.

His biggest affiliation started when Sondra London read Ann Rule's book, *The Stranger Beside Me*, depicting her relationship with Ted Bundy. Sondra thought she could do the same and she requested an audience with Schaefer, whom she had actually dated briefly back in high school. First contact was made on February 8, 1989, to which she received a favorable response from Schaefer. It should be known that Sondra was by that time a struggling true crime author, who was looking for her big break. Her first impression of Schaefer behind bars was that of a "desk bound clerk, middle aged, gone to seed."

Their relationship continued extensively for numerous years, mostly limited to the exchange of stories; which were grisly in nature. In public, Sondra began to attract attention for her conjugal visits to his jail, calling Schaefer a "good friend."

On January 20, 1991, he wrote, "I am the top serial killer and I can prove it." He claimed to be an expert hangman and executioner. "I never at any time required more than two strokes to behead a woman. Never. I was absolutely skilled at it." He estimated his total count of victims ranged between 80 and 110. He claimed, "One whore drowned in her own vomit while watching me disembowel her girlfriend. I'm not sure that counts as a valid kill. Did the pregnant ones count as two kills? It can get confusing." He also claimed that he never used sex as a motive.

By March of 1991, prison officials had become increasingly suspicious of the relationship between Sondra London and Schaefer, and had begun to intercept their mail. He had proposed to London on January 18, 1991, because he knew that if he took her in the confidence of marriage, she could not testify "even if she was shown a basket of severed heads." However, the very next day, he changed his stance. "I will tell you here and now, he wrote, that plenty of your women died because you couldn't help me solve my various crises in 1965. I tried to tell you about it but you couldn't deal with it. You bolted, abandoned me; that's when it started." On May 16, a prison guard found details of another story between the two. A disciplinary report was filed, and as a result, Schaefer spent thirty days in solitary confinement.

For London, book sales had become increasingly stagnant, and as a result she needed new avenues to generate income. She was offered a slot on a TV show for $1,000. While giving an interview to Steve Dunleavy, she said, "He was normal, but with a compulsion to kill." A few days later, in a letter to London, Schaefer wrote, "We are through. You've tapped a black hole of genuine rage and it's focused on you.

Just never speak my name to anyone, anywhere ever again. I've met a number of people from the Satanist Underground. To express my appreciation for what you said on TV, I've explained to them about your daughter. They'll probably get in touch with her personally. If you want to make an issue of this, then the kid is going to be the one to pay on the tab. Am I clear?"

Then, on April 24 in the same year, he again wrote to London, saying he was "prepared to sue everyone. I may not win but I'll break everyone's bank and make the lawyers richer."

London had spent a great deal of time with Schaefer, mainly to get stories out of him that she could write about and generate further income. Their relationship was not sexual in nature, despite the fact that the two had spent a great deal of time together. Schaefer just wasn't interested. For him "sex was not a problem." As Sondra London began to escalate in the world of fame, Schaefer's stock began to rise as well. He began to receive mail from hundreds of groupies from all over the country, asking for his stories.

As mentioned, some women would often visit him to offer him sexual pleasures, which he would turn down. His affliction was with

London, whom he had dated back in high school. In the stories that London published of Schaefer, he claimed he had begun to kill from the early age of nineteen. In 1991, London and Schaefer shared a brief engagement, which she later broke off to get engaged with and married to another serial killer from Florida, by the name of Danny Rolling. The rejection was obviously not well received by Schaefer, who began sending her death threats. He unsuccessfully tried to sue her on multiple occasions for "stealing" his work. Ultimately, Schaefer was killed in his cell in 1995, after his cellmate stabbed him forty-two times and slashed his throat.

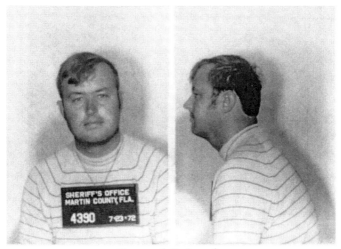

Gerard Schaefer

Sondra London

Continuing with Sondra London's story, one of the most prolific 'serial killer groupies' out there, we now move on to Danny Rolling.

Posing Victims
Danny Rolling

Born on May 26, 1954, Daniel Harold Rolling[xvi] could never have thought that he would one day be referred to as the Gainesville Ripper. Rolling was born in the town of Shreveport, Louisiana. Like many children who grew up to be serial killers, Rolling had a difficult childhood. His father was a police officer of the Shreveport police force, who would often abuse him, his mother Claudia, and his brother Kevin. In one instance, his mother went to the hospital, where she claimed that James Rolling, her husband, had tried to cut her with a razor blade. His mother tried to leave his father a number of times, but she would always come back to him.

Later on, Danny recalled that once, his father exhibited his "cruel sense of discipline" by pinning his hands to the ground, handcuffing him, and then calling the police on him. He kept him pinned like a criminal until the police came to the scene to take him away.

His father had continued to reinforce the idea in his head that he was an "unwanted child" ever since the day he was born. As a result, due to the lack of attention given to him by his parents, Rolling became a distant child and later turned his attention towards robberies, for which he was arrested several times. He was also arrested for spying on a cheerleader as she got dressed. As he grew into adulthood, Rolling began to find it difficult to become a functional member of society, and he was often fired from his job. At some point, Danny Rolling became a waiter at Pancho's Restaurant, which was situated in Shreveport, Louisiana. However, he was fired after failing to show up for work several days in a row.

In May 1990, he attacked his own father with the intention of killing him, during an argument within the family. This attack cost his father his eye and ear. Soon after, Danny Rolling became involved actively in serial killings.

On August 26, 1990, the Gainesville Police Department received a call from a maintenance man regarding loud music. The new school semester was starting, and celebrations had been going round the campus throughout the weekend. When the police officer drove into the Williamsburg Village Apartments on that Sunday afternoon, he was greeted by the maintenance man, who said that a girl's anxious parents were waiting inside because they were unable to locate their daughter and wanted him to open up her apartment for them.

At this time of the year, the police officer wasn't too concerned about a student who may have partied a little too hard and failed to come home. However, when he talked to the parents, Frank and Patricia Powell, he was informed that the parents had told their daughter Christina, who was seventeen years old at the time, that they would be coming over from Jacksonville that Sunday morning, but nobody had seen her since the early hours of Friday. By this point, the police officer had become uneasy. His feeling was compounded when it was found that Christina Powell's roommate, Sonja Larson, also seventeen years old, had not reported to her mother, as had been previously arranged.

Barber,[xvii] the police officer, then told the parents to wait outside, and tried to gain access to the apartment. When he was unable to get through the front door, he broke a glass pane and ventured inside. Almost immediately, a pungent smell engulfed him. There, on the bed, he saw the body of a woman, naked and tied in a grotesque manner with her hands placed over her head. Another young woman's body lay in the stairway on the lower level of the apartment.

Both of the victims had been stabbed repeatedly, their bodies mutilated and positioned to induce the maximum shock effect. Christina Powell had also been raped.

As Barber came out of the apartment, the Powell's worst fears were confirmed. At first impulse, the two wanted to go in and see their daughter, but Barber told them it was best for all parties concerned if they didn't. A double homicide was called in from the Alachua Crisis Center, and so began the investigation into the killings of Danny Rolling.

One day later, another murder was called in. This time, Rolling had broken into the apartment of one Christa Hoyt, using a knife and a screwdriver. Upon finding that the girl was not home, he waited for her return. At 11:00 a.m., Christa entered the apartment. He surprised her from behind by placing her in a chokehold, subduing her. He then taped her wrists together, and placed duct tape on her mouth as well. He then cut her clothes, and proceeded to rape her. When he was done, he put her face down, and stabbed her straight in the back, causing her heart to rupture. He then decapitated her and positioned the head to face the corpse, resulting in a horrible crime scene.

By this point in time, widespread media attention had been attracted towards the killings, and students had become aware of what was happening. They had also begun to take precautions, sleeping in groups, and making sure to barricade their doors. Tracy Paules was living with Manny Taboada, her 200-pound roommate. Danny Rolling broke into their apartment, killing Taboada after a brief struggle. As Paules tried to barricade herself in the room, he broke in, taped her wrists and mouth, raped her, and then killed her by stabbing in the same manner as before. He also took the time to pose Paules' body, but left Taboada's untouched.

It was perhaps by accident that Rolling was even captured. The police only had a handful of leads, and were initially investigating another person altogether. However, Rolling was arrested on a burglary charge, and his tools matched the ones suspected of being used in the Gainesville murders. Danny Rolling was officially arrested, and several charges of first-degree murder were levied against him.

By this time, Sondra London was becoming more and more disenchanted with Gerard John Schaefer. He was unwilling to disclose more information regarding his cases, while her book sales were becoming more and more stagnant. Desperate for new material, she had begun granting interviews on television, but the money she made from them simply wasn't enough to pay her bills. Rolling's case had already begun to attract significant attention from the media, and London wanted a new story. It was a perfect match. But by 1991, London and Schaefer were already engaged. She soon broke it off to pursue a new story and potential relationship with Rolling. While Rolling had received support from certain groupies, his fan base was nowhere near as big as that of other killers, such as Ted Bundy, Gerard John Schaefer, or others we have discussed in this book.

In May of 1992, Rolling was transferred to the Florida State Prison, and placed in the psych ward for evaluation. This was because of the continuous suicide attempts that Rolling had tried on himself, along with a number of episodes relating to violent behavior. At the Florida State Prison, apart from carrying out his daily duties in prison, Rolling would spend some time exercising, writing letters and songs, as well as making drawings. Sondra London first tested the waters to analyze whether he was literate enough to understand and write well (mainly because she thrived on the writings of serial killers) by using a pseudonym to write to him. When she finally contacted him using her real name, she didn't reveal that she had talked to him before. By this point, Sondra had begun to refer to herself as the 'media queen' of inmate literature.

For Sondra, her main source of income was to share stories and drawings made by inmates on death row. At first, the two began their relationship in a purely professional manner— Rolling would share his stories, while Sondra would publish them, ultimately making him famous. However, it wasn't very long before both London and Rolling were proclaiming their love for each other to the public. Letters soon began to be intercepted by the prison guards, which were used by the prosecution, and excerpts from the letters began to appear in *The Gainesville Sun*, which showed how London was trying to coax Rolling into revealing explicit details of the murders.

Rolling's parents, along with others, highlighted their concern that Sondra London was only using Rolling to her own advantage. However, Rolling refuted the claim. He wrote, "I love her and it cuts me deeply to know there are people out there who have caused her pain because she finds something in Danny Rolling to love." Together, the couple published a book, entitled *The Making of a Serial Killer: The Real Story of the Gainesville Murders.*[xviii] The book included a number of capital crimes that prosecutors had not even charged him with. The book also included around fifty pictures that had been drawn by hand by Danny Rolling during his time in prison. The two remained engaged for a number of years, and may or may not have married. Danny Rolling was served justice however, as he was put to rest by lethal injection back in 2006. Sondra London still continues to write inmate literature.

Danny Rolling

Kenneth Alessio Bianchi[xix] was born on May 22, 1951. His cousin, Angelo Buono, Jr.,[xx] was born on October 5, 1934. When Kenneth was twenty-six and his cousin was forty-three, the two went out on a rampage, and were dubbed by the media as the 'Hillside Stranglers.' Here's their story:

Kenneth Bianchi was born in Rochester, New York. His mother was a prostitute, and because Bianchi was likely going to get in the way of her profession, his mother put him up for adoption a couple of weeks after he was born. He was soon adopted by his new parents, Frances Scioliono and her husband Nicholas Bianchi. From a very young age, Bianchi showed signs of being deeply troubled. In the words of his own mother, she said Bianchi was a "compulsive liar who had risen from the cradle dissembling." Bianchi often went through trance like daydreams, which worried his mother very much. Compared to other students of his age, Bianchi had above average intelligence, but despite that fact, he was often very quick to lose his temper. At the tender age of just five years old, Bianchi was diagnosed with petit mal seizures, and by the time he was ten, he was diagnosed with passive-aggressive disorder.

His father died of pneumonia when he was just ten years of age, in the year 1964. As a result, his mother would go off to work while Kenneth would attend high school. The neighbors later on noted that his mother Frances would keep him home from school for long periods of time, just to be with him. Young Bianchi also had a urination problem, and he made frequent visits to the doctor. Because the doctors would examine his genitals in detail in order to get to the root of the problem, he often felt quite humiliated.

Bianchi attended the Gates-Chili High School in his teenage years, and upon graduating in the year 1971, he tied the knot with his childhood sweetheart. However, the marriage was short-lived, as their union ended after just eight months. It was rumored that his bride simply left him without giving an explanation. Bianchi then enrolled in college, but found he didn't quite fit into the group of students there. As a result of being unable to assimilate himself into the crowd, he dropped out of college just one semester later.

From there on, Bianchi moved from one menial job to another, until finally he found employment as a security guard at a jewelry store. As a result, this gave him unprecedented access to the store, allowing him to steal valuables whenever he wanted. Often times, he would gift these valuables to his girlfriends or prostitutes in order to gain their trust and loyalty. Because of the sheer number of petty thefts that he would be involved in, Bianchi was constantly on the move from one place to another.

In the year 1977, twenty-six-year-old Bianchi moved to Los Angeles. The main factor behind his moving from New York to Los Angeles was the fact that he had begun spending time with his older cousin, Angel Buono. Bianchi was visibly impressed by Buono, who wore fancy clothes and jewelry, and who had a penchant for getting "any woman he wanted and then putting them in their place." It wasn't very long before Bianchi became a sort of understudy to Buono, and the two began working as pimps, which ultimately led to murder.

***

Angelo Buono was also born in Rochester, New York, to first generation emigrants who had settled in New York from San Buono, Italy. By the time he began to kill, Buono was already known amongst the police force, mainly because he had accumulated a number of arrests and a substantial record of criminal history. Some of the charges against him included failure to pay child support, as well as grand theft auto, full assault, and rape. It was in 1975, when he was forty-one years of age, when Buono got in touch with his cousin Bianchi.

Buono would often refer to himself as the "ladies' man," and he coaxed Bianchi into prostituting a couple of women, keeping them as virtual prisoners. He would often force women to refer to him as 'The Italian Stallion.' By the time that the two were arrested, the pair had raped and subsequently murdered ten women.

Commonly, the duo would cruise around the city of Los Angeles in Bianchi's car, and would make use of fake badges in order to persuade young girls into thinking that they were undercover cops. They would then ask the women to get into their 'unmarked' car, and would drive them home, where the women would be raped and murdered after.

The victims[xxi] included women from all walks of life, ranging from the ages of twelve years old up to twenty-eight. Here's a brief list of their victims:

- **Yolanda Washington**, age nineteen, murdered on October 17, 1977;
- **Judith Lynn Miller**, age fifteen, murdered on October 31, 1977;
- **Lissa Kastin**, age twenty-one, murdered on November 6, 1977;
- **Jane King**, age twenty-eight, murdered on November 10, 1977;
- **Dolores Cepeda**, age twelve, murdered on November 13, 1977;
- **Sonja Johnson**, age fourteen, murdered on November 13, 1977;
- **Kristina Weckler**, age twenty, murdered on November 20, 1977;
- **Lauren Wagner**, age eighteen, murdered on November 29, 1977;
- **Kimberely Martin**, age seventeen, murdered on December 9, 1977;
- **Cindy Lee Hudspeth**, age twenty, murdered on February 16, 1978;
- **Karen Mandic**, age twenty-two, murdered on January 11, 1979; and

- **Diane Wilder**, age twenty-seven, murdered on January 11, 1979.

Before strangling their victims, both of the men would first rape the women. Horribly, they also tried other methods of killing their victims, such as electric shocks, poisoning by carbon monoxide, as well as lethal injections. During the time the two were committing the murders, Bianchi had applied for a job with the Los Angeles Police Department, and ironically, even embarked on a number of 'ride-alongs' in a police cruiser as they searched for what the media referred to as the 'Hillside Strangler.' Little did the police know at the time that killer was, in fact, two men.

One night, just after that two had managed to screw up their 'eleventh' murder, Bianchi told Buono that he had embarked on several ride-alongs with the Los Angeles Police Department, and that he was also on the list of questioning suspects regarding the case of the Hillside Strangler. Upon hearing this, Buono erupted. An argument soon began between the two, and Buono subsequently threatened Bianchi, stating that he would kill him if he did not leave the city and head to Bellingham,

Washington. Bianchi became fearful, and in May of 1978, he did run off to Bellingham.

On January 11, 1979, while working as a security guard, Bianchi coaxed two women into the house that he was supposed to be guarding. One of them was twenty-two years old and the other was twenty-seven years old. Their names were Karen Mandic and Diane Wilder, respectively. Both were students at Western Washington University. He forced Mandic down the stairs in front of him, and then strangled her. Diane Wilder met the same fate. However, this time, Bianchi did not have the help from his partner, who was older and more experienced when it came to hiding the murders and making sure that no traces were left behind. As a result, Bianchi left a number of clues at the crime scene. Police were able to apprehend him the very next day. A driver's license from California, along with a standard background check revealed a link between the victims of the 'Hillside Strangler' and Bianchi.

As soon as he was arrested, Bianchi began to spill the beans. He revealed how Buono and he had started killing together two years prior, back in 1977, while posing as police officers. He also revealed they had once abducted a woman named Catharine Lorre, with the intention of killing her. However, when they learned that Catharine Lorre was the daughter of famed actor Peter Lorre, they'd let her go. It wasn't until the time that Bianchi was arrested when Catharine Lorre learned about how she had virtually escaped from a brutal, gruesome death.

Kenny Bianchi told the police of how Angelo Buono had acted as a strong role model for him. He also taught Bianchi how to get a prostitute for free by just flashing a badge in her face. "You can't let a c**t get the upper hand. Put them in their place," Angelo had instructed Kenny. Bianchi told the police that the first two prostitutes that they had initially held as prisoners went by the names of Sabra Hannan and Becky Spears. They forced the girls to prostitute themselves, or else be subjected to torturous physical punishment. When Becky met David Wood, an attorney by profession, she told him what she was going through. David Wood decided to arrange an escape for Becky out of the city. When Buono found out, he threatened Wood. Unfortunately, Wood had connections in high places, and one call was enough to convince Angelo to back down.

Becky's escape had a strong impact upon Sabra, who planned her own escape a short while later. She soon ran away after Becky's escape. But, after both prostitutes had escaped, Angelo and Kenny were not getting any income from their pimping. As a result, Bianchi began missing out on payments for his Cadillac. Soon after, the Cadillac was repossessed. They knew that more teenage girls were needed. Yolanda Washington and Deborah Noble were two prostitutes who delivered a 'trick list' to the two, which contained names of clients who were frequent to visit prostitutes. When it was found that the list was a fake handed to them by Deborah Noble (told to them by Yolanda Washington), they became enraged, and Yolanda Washington was the first to die by their hands.

Amazingly, you could call Kenny a lot of things, but stupid wasn't one of them. While he was locked up in the Whatcom County Jail in Bellingham, he was able to convince Dean Brett, his lawyer appointed by court, that he was suffering from amnesia. Dean Brett became deeply concerned for his client's welfare, and called in a psychiatric social worker to talk to Kenny. The psychiatric social worker was at first confused. Kenny appeared to be mild in his manners, and soft- spoken. Hence, he came to the conclusion that Kenny was suffering from a multiple personality disorder. There really was no other plausible explanation. This was the break that Kenny needed. He got to work, and laid the foundations of a truly hair-raising scam. He had seen the movie *The Three Faces of Eve* a few years ago, and he used the small amount of knowledge that he gained from studying psychology in concocting a plan.

Luck aided him, as just before his interview, he saw *Sybil*, a movie that depicted multiple personality disorders. He was able to convince a few expert psychiatrists that he was suffering from a multiple personality disorder. However, investigators weren't fully convinced, and called in their own psychiatrist, which is how Martin Orne entered into the story. Orne let it slip that whenever there are genuine cases of this type of disorder, there are commonly more than a couple of personalities that are adopted by the person. Previously, Kenny had only been posing as 'Steve Walker.' Soon after, he created the alias 'Billy.' Investigators working behind the scenes soon discovered that 'Steve Walker' was in fact a student, whose identity Kenneth had tried to steal so that he could become a practicing psychiatrist in a fraudulent manner. The police also found a small stash of books in

Bianchi's home, which focused mainly on topics of modern psychology.

All of this pointed to one thing: he had to be faking the disorder. Soon, all of his claims were put under scrutiny, and Martin Orne clarified that he was fit to stand trial. Eventually, Bianchi admitted to creating the fake identities in order to create the "façade of a disorder." However, he was ultimately diagnosed with antisocial personality disorder, along with sexual sadism. Now, Kenny knew that his actions could ultimately lead to the death penalty. As a result, he wanted to gain some leniency, and decided to testify against his own cousin.

In 1982, *People v. Buono* started in earnest. Numerous women, who claimed to be 'admirers' of the duo, attended the trial. Despite the fact that Buono was an ugly man physically, the courtroom was crowded. A number of witnesses arrived to testify, including the women that they had brutalized, including Becky Spears and Sabra Hannan. When Kenny's turn came to testify, he initially refused to cooperate, but finally relented when reminded of the brutal conditions in which he would be spending the remainder of his life. Despite that, most of the statements that Bianchi gave were contradictory in themselves, as he wanted to avoid getting Buono convicted because of him.

It was the longest trial in the history of the United States at the time, and the jury finally came to the conclusion that Angel Buono and Kenneth Bianchi be subjected to life imprisonment. The judge was unhappy at the verdict. He stated, "Angelo Buono and Kenneth Bianchi subjected various of their murder victims to the administration of lethal gas, electrocution, strangulation by rope, and lethal hypodermic injection. Yet the two defendants are destined to spend their lives in prison, housed, fed, and clothed at taxpayer expense, better cared for than some of the destitute law-abiding members of our community."

Both Angel Buono and Kenneth Bianchi had their own respective groupies that we shall now talk about.

In 1986, while he was incarcerated in prison, Angel Buono married Christine Kizuka, a mother of three children. She was a supervisor at the Los Angeles Office of the State Employment Development Department. Kizuka met Buono through her first husband, who spent a total of five months in a cell that was located right next to Buono's. She divorced him in May of 1983, just three years before she married

Buono. Because of the horrific nature of crimes that he had committed against women, prison officials were quick to go on record and state that no conjugal visits would ever be allowed.

And now, we move on to Veronica Compton. All that has been written about Kenneth Bianchi gives a clear indication of his state of mind, and yet, if you'd deem Bianchi 'crazy,' I wonder how you would see Veronica Compton. At the time when Bianchi and Buono hit the headlines, Compton had been busy writing a play about a female serial killer, which she aptly named *The Mutilated Cutter*. As soon as she heard about Bianchi, she wanted to talk to him so as to get a better idea of what went on in the mind of a serial killer. It didn't take her very long to completely fall in love with Bianchi.

For Kenny, this relationship served as a small outlet. He knew that Compton was completely willing to do whatever he wanted her to do. Kenneth Bianchi then made a shocking proposal to Compton. He knew that if she accepted the proposal and did what he asked, Kenneth would be freed for life, which would mean that "he could spend the rest of his life with Compton." What was the proposal? Kenneth asked Compton to travel to

Bellingham and then strangle a girl, and then make it seem as if it was the same person who had killed Diane Wilder and Karen Mandic. He asked her to perhaps even get some semen and plant it on the dead body. Any other person would have balked at this, but Veronica Compton wasn't any other person; she accepted the request.

In the days before DNA testing was conducted, Kenny's blood type was unable to be determined using his semen. As a result, Kenny sent Veronica off on her way, after giving her a fresh load of his semen in a plastic glove. However, the project was slightly more intimidating than she had initially thought it would be. Therefore, upon arrival in Bellingham, to boost up her courage, Veronica had to consume lots of alcohol, as well as cocaine.

Once her mind became numb to all morality, Veronica ventured out, and managed to lure a woman into driving her to a motel, and then called her in for a drink. When they were in the security of the room, Veronica tried to strangle the woman using a cord. However, she had not anticipated that the woman would be stronger than her. The woman threw Veronica off and ran. Veronica came to the conclusion that it was time to head back to California. However, her mind was only rational for a few moments, and when she arrived at the airport, she was hysterical, creating a scene that was noticed by numerous people.

In what can only be described as utter stupidity, Veronica wrote a letter and sent it along with a tape to the authorities at Bellingham that an innocent man had been arrested, and then stated that the recent strangling attempt was proof enough that the real culprit was very much at large. Needless to say, the police didn't have to comb through a great deal of reports or spend sleepless nights pondering over her picture and the description of the woman who had created a scene at the airport to realize that they were both the same.

Now that Kenneth Bianchi knew that Veronica could not be relied upon in the future, his 'love' for her cooled down significantly. He eventually married another woman, by the name of Shirlee Joyce Book, who was thirty-six years old at the time. She hailed from Monterey, Los Angeles. The ceremony was held in the prison chapel, and the bride wore a proper white dress along with a small veil, while Bianchi wore a black tuxedo.

As a result, Compton focused her attention on a new man, Douglas Clark, another convicted serial killer, who made Bianchi seem like a player from the lower leagues. Kenny's loss proved to be Clark's gain. Now, both were in jail. Here's a small excerpt of what Veronica once wrote to Clark: "I take out my straight razor and with one quick stroke I slit the veins in the crook of your arm. Your blood spurts out and spits atop my swelled breasts. Then later that night we cuddle in each other's arms before the fireplace and dress each other's wound with kisses and loving caresses."

Veronica Compton

Buono and Bianchi

Next we'll discuss the story of Douglas Clark and Carol M. Bundy (who is not related to Ted Bundy in any way).

Douglas Daniel Clark[xxii] was born on March 10, 1948. Because he was born to a Naval Intelligence Officer (Franklin Clark), his family was often on the move, due to the nature of his father's work. Later on, when he was arrested, Clark claimed that he had lived in thirty-seven different countries across the globe.

When Clark was ten years old, in 1958, his father opted out of the Navy, and instead chose to work in a civilian position as an engineer, subsequently joining the Transport Company of Texas. Still, the family lived like nomads, constantly moving from one place to another. For some time, the family lived in the Marshall Islands, and then moved to San Francisco. From there on, they moved to India. For a short span of time, Douglas Clark studied in an exclusive international school along with the children of rich men in Geneva. Later on, he attended the Culver Military Academy.

In the meanwhile, his father continued to travel from one place to another. Upon graduating in the year 1967, Clark chose to enlist in the Air Force. He would often refer to himself as "the king of one-night stands," as he engaged in many sexual exploits with underage girls and young women. However, in his private time, thoughts of rape and murder would consume him, and dark fantasies of mutilation and necrophilia would begin to form in the deepest crevices of his mind. He yearned for the moment when he would graduate, so that he could bring his fantasies into the real world.

***

Carol Bundy[xxiii] was born August 26, 1947, and like many of the serial killers that we have discussed here, she also suffered through a troubled childhood. At a very young age, her mother succumbed to death, while her father continued to abuse her. When her father decided to remarry, poor Carol was placed in numerous foster homes. At the tender age of seventeen, Bundy married a fifty-six-year-old man. Perhaps this gives a clear indication of the disturbed mental state that the young nurse was in. She soon became overweight and her eyesight deteriorated tremendously.

In 1979, however, she left her husband, and soon after fell in love with the manager of her apartment building. John Murray, who was a native of Australia, was a part time singer in a local western country bar. Regardless of his commitments, John would always find time to help out tenants who needed his help.

When he noticed that Carol suffered from severe cataracts, he elected to drive her to a Social Security Office. There, he helped her to declare herself to be legally blind, which allowed Carol to bring in a sum of $620 in welfare benefits for herself and her sons. From there, he took her to an optometrist, where she got new glasses, and finally discarded the white cane that she would often be seen carrying around with her. For Carol, this was a completely new experience and she had never had a man care for her in such a manner before. She became enraptured. Then, she started thinking of ways to bring him over to her apartment however she could; often by clogging the toilets and the drains within her apartment. Soon, the two fell in love. However, there was a slight problem: John Murray was married, and he did not leave his family behind.

Then, in October, Bundy made a foolish move; she approached Murray's wife, and offered the lady her savings, which totaled around $1,500, in exchange for the woman leaving Murray and disappearing. Obviously, her attempt backfired on her, and Murray berated her before his wife, and then suggested that she find lodging elsewhere. In January of 1980, three months later, while sitting in a country-western bar called Little Nashville, Carol met Douglas Clark.[xxiv] He made her feel like a princess. Ironically, the reason why she was in a country western bar was because she was still infatuated with John Murray, and was listening to him sing. On the very same night, Douglas Clark moved in with Carol Bundy, and so began a deadly affiliation between the two.

Clark had been discharged from the Air Force a decade earlier, and had been drifting around from one job to another, sometimes working as a mechanic. When he moved to Los Angeles, he found employment as a boiler operator in a Jergens soap factory in Burbank. However, he was fired soon after because of the sheer number of absences on his report, coupled with the numerous threats that he levied against his coworkers within the factory. Each night, he would make Carol feel out of this world, until she was completely enslaved to him. Hence, when Clark started to bring home younger women to fulfill his sexual fantasies, Carol did not mind too much. When her pride did begin to come to the fore, she would often hurriedly change the subject.

She was enraptured by Clark, and when commanded, would dutifully take as many pictures as asked of him with other women. It did not take long for kinky sex to pave the way for pedophilia, and Clark's next interest became an eleven-year-old girl, who was also their neighbor. With the help of Bundy, Clark was able to lure the girl into their house while she was skating in a nearby park, and then started playing 'sexual games' with her while Bundy snapped 'sexual photographs.' Often times, Bundy would actively participate as well. At night, their discussions would be increasingly punctuated by dark fantasies, and both would indulge the other in twisted, sadistic tales that brewed in the darkest corners of their minds. Pedophilia didn't prove to be enough for either of them, and soon Clark expressed a desire to kill a girl during sexual intercourse. Ultimately, he managed to convince Bundy to buy a couple of automatic pistols for which he could use to perform the kill. In a later report, it was detailed that Clark had a fantasy of killing a woman during sex, and then feeling the contractions in her vagina as her body underwent death spasms.

The killings[xxv] began in mid-June 1980. On June 11, half sisters Gina Narano and Cynthia Chandler, fifteen and sixteen years of age respectively, went missing without a trace from Huntington Beach after they headed out to meet their friends. Their bodies were found by a California Department of Transportation (Caltrans) worker, who was picking up trash near the embankments on the Ventura Highway. One of the bodies was nude, while the other was clad in a pink jumpsuit, and both of them had been shot directly in the head with a small caliber weapon.

There was no ID on either of them, and because of the hours that the bodies had spent in the sun, they had become bloated. Incredibly, this was the same place where Yolanda Washington had been killed and her body had been dumped by Buono and Bianchi. The police were also clear of the fact that the killer wasn't concerned whether the bodies were found or not; they were both left in plain view.

According to reports, Douglas Clark had ordered both the girls to perform fellatio on him, and as they heeded his command, he had shot both of them in the head, and then taken their bodies to the garage, where he raped the dead bodies, and then dumped them. He then relayed his exploits to Carol Bundy, who became uneasy at the news. Soon after, a call was received at the police station from a woman

(Bundy), who said that her boyfriend had committed the murders, but she would not help the policemen in disclosing his location. For all they knew, it could have been a prank caller. However, Bundy revealed details that had not been released by the police to the media. But, for unknown reasons, the switchboard cut her off. Had she been allowed to continue, a number of other lives could have been saved. Alas, it was not to be.

A week and five days passed until Clark struck again, but this time, Bundy refrained from contacting the police. Both the victims this time were prostitutes by the name of Exxie Wilson and Karen Jones. Clark's *modus operandi* remained the same; he lured the two prostitutes into his car, shot them both and then dumped the bodies in plain sight. However, this time around, there was a slight variation in his methods. He took home a token of his work: the head of Exxie Wilson. After bringing the head back home, he placed it in the fridge. When Bundy saw the head in the fridge, she put makeup on it, and then Clark proceeded to perform "another bout of necrophilia." A couple of days later, Bundy and Clark teamed up to throw away the head in an alleyway. Later on, Bundy recalled that time, saying, "we had a lot of fun with her. I was making her up like a Barbie with makeup."

Three days passed. Then, a group of snake hunters were busy in search of their prey in the San Fernando Valley, when they found something that none of them would ever forget for the rest of their lives—a woman's corpse that had been mummified from top to bottom. They immediately phoned the authorities, and subsequent checks revealed the body belonged to Marnette Comer. She was a seventeen-year-old prostitute, and had been dead for a minimum of three weeks before her body was found. The murders continued.

Meanwhile, Bundy's anger at John Murray had not subsided. She would still venture to hear him sing at the Little Nashville bar. But after a few drinks, their conversation would often turn awry, as Bundy would begin to detail the things that she and Clark were doing. Murray was horrified, and let it slip that he may inform the police. Bundy became scared at this prospect, because she wasn't planning on getting caught anytime soon. So, she created a ruse; she invited him for sex in his van in August of 1980. Once they were safely inside, she shut the door, and then shot him straight in the head. Afterwards, she decapitated him.

However, she was inexperienced in the art of killing as yet, and ultimately left a number of clues behind; many witnesses reported that Murray had last been seen walking out of the bar with her, while she also forgot the shell casings within the vehicle.

Unlike Clark, Bundy found it difficult to operate under pressure and just a couple of days later, spilled the beans to her co-workers about her role in Murray's killing. The police were called in immediately, and Bundy gave a complete confession regarding all of the crimes that she and Douglas Clark had committed. Soon after, Douglas Clark was arrested, and the weapons were found hidden at his workplace.

During the trial, Clark tried to make it seem as if Bundy was the reason for all that had happened, and portrayed himself as an innocent "dupe." The jury paid little heed to whatever he said, and he was subsequently sentenced to death in 1983. He is currently on death row. For her role in capturing Clark by disclosing crucial information to the police, Bundy was able to cut a plea bargain, which meant that she avoided the death penalty and instead received imprisonment for life. Carol Bundy succumbed to her death due to heart failure back in 2003.

When Douglas Clark realized that Veronica Compton was now sharing a cell with his ex-girlfriend Carol Bundy, he set about to impress her. He began sending her love letters and flowers, along with grisly drawings of beheaded women. The two soon became intertwined, and began sharing plans of opening a mortuary together, so that they could both gain unrestricted access to dead bodies, which they could disrespect further. He even convinced Compton to testify at his trial that all of the killings were masterminded by Carol Bundy only. However, as it had happened before, Compton again failed spectacularly under pressure, and pleaded the Fifth on the stand. Soon after, things began to turn sour for the two lovebirds and Clark began to threaten her.

Ultimately, Compton managed to escape from prison, but decided against her move, and returned back. Upon her release, Compton ended up marrying an older professor who was a teacher at the prison.

Doug Clark and Carol Bundy

Epilogue

There are hundreds, if not thousands of women who write to these serial killers on a regular basis. A criminal psychologist by the name of Frank Colistro[xxvi] stated that serial killers "often radiate a perverse charisma" that is found to be highly attractive by groupies. Providing an explanation, Colistro said, "A lot of them get caught up in the drama that's associated with these people forever."

"You do get a lot of inadequate, insecure women," Colistro said. "In a sense, they're the perfect boyfriend, the perfect husband. In a sense, you can do a relationship light, so to speak."

There are numerous websites, such as writeaprisoner.com or romanticjailbabes.com, which allow individuals to provide assistance to women who wish to get in touch with men behind bars.

It should be known that these women, once they become romantically involved with inmates, devote themselves totally to the inmate, and even end up making a number of different sacrifices, the most obvious of which is the fact that they are willing to sit for hours on end, just so that they can get a brief face to face visit with that inmate in prison. Many women, some of whom we have already discussed, have left their jobs and their families, moving from one place to another just so that they could be near these inmates. It goes without saying that these women also spend money on them, sometimes until all of their savings are depleted.

They fail to realize that they are just pawns for these men, who often meet with numerous enamored women apart from their 'lovers.' Perhaps one of the main reasons why groupies are so attracted towards inmates who are on death row is because they have a distinct allure that comes from killing a person and being found guilty of it, and because they are condemned.

Websites such as writeaprisoner.com even provide direct advice and recommend the general public to write to these inmates. Some say that they offer a convincing argument. The following few lines are taken directly from www.writeaprisoner.com,[xxvii] so decide for yourself:

1. Without such contact with society outside the prison walls, rehabilitation would be adversely

affected, prison morale weakened, perhaps inviting riots and other forms of internal disorder.

2. It may provide an incentive to lower recidivism.

3. Returning prisoners who were employed after release relied largely on personal connections—family, friends, former employers—to find their jobs

4. Spiritual satisfaction is guaranteed for the writer.

Importantly, a simple study into the interests of these serial killer groupies reveals that the profile of the serial killer should not necessarily mean that he is an attractive person. Henry Lee Lucas was one-eyed and confessed to more than 300 murders, and despite the fact that he gave horrific details regarding his actions, he still managed to get a huge number of female admirers. Despite the fact that he had an ostensibly sexual relationship with Ottis Toole, another murderer, some women still find him to be attractive enough to be a potential mate to them.

One of his many admirers even came up with a plan to free him, supposedly by acting as his former girlfriend whom he had murdered. It is utterly disrespectful to the victims, but this sort of thing happens.

Yet another example is that of John Wayne Gacy, a man who killed more than thirty-three young men, all during homosexual encounters. John Wayne Gacy was overweight, a big whiner, and a complete narcissist. He married in prison.

There are countless other examples, all of which point to the conclusion that good looks are not the only requisite to attract attention from female admirers while in prison. Many women have stated that they actively search FBI websites in order to find criminals who have been recently incarcerated, so that they can begin writing to them. Most of these women just carry out cursory searches of their actions, which gives them a clear idea of how notorious the inmate really is. After all, it is unlikely that a person would be on death row for a simple case of vandalism.

Rosalie Martinez, a mitigation specialist and public defender, was once happily married to a person also hailing from a similar profession— an attorney. The couple had four beautiful daughters. Little did her husband know how rapidly things would change.

Their whole life fell apart when Rosalie met Oscar Ray Bolin Jr. In 1995, she left her husband for a person who was on death row. The two married in the same year, over a telephone call.

Oscar Ray Bolin Jr. was a former carnival worker. He was found guilty of raping ten women, and was convicted ten times for it, as well as for the murder of three women in Florida, whom he brutally stabbed repeatedly until they died. While he was already on death row for two death sentences, he received another life sentence. In every case that he was convicted, the rulings were overturned due to errors. Each time, he was granted a retrial, and each time he was convicted again. He killed a twenty-six-year-old, a seventeen-year-old, and one other girl during the year 1986. Rosalie Martinez, however, is under the impression that Martinez is not a killer.

She once said that upon meeting him for the first time, she was left "breathless." She said that she could sense how "isolated and lonely" he was. Speaking to a reporter, she said, "It affected me because I felt the same way." Imagine how her husband must have felt. According to her, the only reason why she decided to marry him was because she wanted to raise awareness "of the injustice of his plight." Many of these women who are mainly attracted to serial killers are usually those who are well into their thirties or forties. Despite the fact that the motives for being in the relationship might vary, all of them share a strong sense of protection over the relationship itself. Some of the women know that their incarcerated love interest is guilty of heinous crimes, but others are blinded, openly believing that the person they are in love with is innocent, even though there is clear evidence to state otherwise.

For many of you reading this, you might be thinking that these relationships defy common sense. And in all likelihood, they do. However, numerous theorists have tried to create a hypothetical biological impetus that is operational, apart from the logical explanation that might accompany such a relationship. Extensive research into primates has revealed that the female inherently prefers the larger, more aggressive and the louder male; in short, those males who are able to provide a clear marker of their maleness. Compared to humans, certain women might believe that a male who is aggressive might be able to provide more in all aspects as compared to an ordinary man.

Subconsciously, by being with him, or devoting herself to him, she is able to gain a sense of protection and status. Regardless of the psychological standpoint, it is common in prisons that the most dangerous males often draw in the most amount of women who will all be hoping to one day become his wife, despite the fact that they would never be able to live together.

There have been countless different studies, along with substantial evidence that can be found from web searches, which reveal that women show an extremely robust erotic preference towards men who are more dominant. In common terminology, this is referred to as the alpha male. On a conscious level, women would want to choose a man who is kind, respects them and others, and is also understanding and empathic. However, it is common knowledge that women are deeply attracted to 'bad boys.' Hence, when they have an option of being engaged with a bad boy, while making sure that they remain safe (the killers are usually kept behind bars), these women do not mind taking up that option. We have already discussed how so many find the notion of being with a man on trial or incarcerated to be so pleasurable, just because they believe they now have the perfect boyfriend.

Throughout history, there have been countless serial killers who have attracted women to their trials, and a great number of these men end up happily marrying these women. Most of the marriage ceremonies are held in prison chapels, with only a handful of people in attendance.

Amazingly, the women who marry these men make sure that they carry out all of the rituals, such as wearing a white dress with a veil, and cutting a small cake, etc. However, there is a trade-off. These men are outcasts of society. They are rejected, and deserve to spend the remainder of their lives in prison.

The women, however, are typically not incarcerated, and as a result, have to bear the constant demands of society. Often times when these women marry these men, they leave behind their families, as people usually tend to break contact with women who are affiliated with such horrendous men.

While most of these serial killer groupies openly admit that they are under no illusions regarding the dangerous nature of the man they have committed their life to, many of them are under the impression that they are innocent.

While others, such as Veronica Compton, seem to find a partner who shares the same sadistic thinking that they do.

A Facebook friend, Pam Olsen, recently commented on one of my posts about this topic that maybe these women should be writing and reaching out to soldiers, victims and survivors of crime. I think it's a valid point.

Newly released True Crime Books
by RJ Parker Publishing, Inc.

Social Media Monsters: Internet Killers
by JJ Slate and RJ Parker
September 18, 2014

Who is really on the other end of that Facebook friend request, or behind that dating profile, or posting that item for sale on Craigslist? How can you be safe if you plan to meet up with a stranger you met online? What precautions should you take?

In this book, we have detailed more than thirty chilling true stories of killers that have used the internet to locate, stalk, lure, or exploit their victims. Facebook, Craigslist, MySpace, chat rooms, dating sites—it does not matter where you are online; killers are lurking in the shadows. They lurk in suicide chat rooms, search for escorts on Craigslist, and create fake social media profiles to fool and gain the trust of their victims. Someone you have been talking to for months or even years could be a completely different person from what you envisioned.

Serial Killers True Crime Anthology: Vol II 2015
by Katherine Ramsland, Sylvia Perrini, Kelly Banaski, Michael Newton, Peter Vronsky, and RJ Parker
December 15, 2014

In the 2nd annual Serial Killers True Crime Anthology, five acclaimed true crime authors presents some of the worst, and recent cases of serial homicide, including:

Joanna Dennehy
Enriqueta Marti
Douglas and Donna Perry
Brian Dugan
The Oakland County Child Killer
The Truck Stop Serial Killers
Rosemary West
Don Harvey
Michael Swango
Lonnie Franklin
Harold Shipman
Michael McCray
David Russell Williams

Missing Wives, Missing Lives
by JJ Slate
June 16, 2014

When a wife goes missing, her husband is often the prime suspect in her disappearance. But what happens when she is never found? In some of the cases profiled in this chilling book, the husbands were found guilty of murder, even without a body.

Missing Wives, Missing Lives focuses on thirty unique cases in which the wife has never been found and the undying efforts of her family as they continue the painful search to bring her home. The book covers decades old cases, such as Jeanette Zapata, who has been missing since 1976, to more recent and widely known cases, such as Stacy Peterson, who has been missing since 2007. Keeping these women's stories alive may be the key to solving the mystery and bringing them home to their family.

Parents Who Killed their Children: Filicide
by RJ Parker
April 30, 2014

What could possibly incite parents to kill their own children?

This collection of "Filicidal Killers" provides a gripping overview of how things can go horribly wrong in once-loving families. *Parents Who Killed their Children* depicts ten of the most notorious and horrific cases of homicidal parental units out of control. People like Andrea Yates, Diane Downs, Susan Smith, and Jeffrey MacDonald, who received a great deal of media attention. The author explores the reasons behind these murders; from addiction to postpartum psychosis, insanity to altruism.

Each story is detailed with background information on the parents, the murder scenes, trials, sentencing and aftermath.

The Vampire Next Door:
The True Story of the Vampire Rapist
by JT Hunter
October 11, 2014

John Crutchley seemed to be living the American Dream. Good-looking and blessed with a genius level IQ, he had a prestigious, white-collar job at a prominent government defense contractor, where he held top-secret security clearance and handled projects for NASA and the Pentagon. To all outward appearances, he was a hard-working, successful family man with a lavish new house, a devoted wife, and a healthy young son.

But, he concealed a hidden side of his personality, a dark secret tied to a hunger for blood and the overriding need to kill. As one of the most prolific serial killers in American history, Crutchley committed at least twelve murders, and possibly nearly three dozen. His IQ eclipsed that of Ted Bundy, and his body count may have as well. While he stalked the streets hunting his unsuspecting victims, the residents of a quiet Florida town slept soundly, oblivious to the dark creature in their midst, unaware of the vampire next door.

Serial Killers Abridged:
An Encyclopedia of 100 Serial Killers
by RJ Parker
May 31, 2014

WARNING: There are dramatic crime scene photos in this book that some may find very disturbing

The ultimate reference for anyone compelled by the pathologies and twisted minds behind the most disturbing of homicidal monsters. From A to Z, there are names you may not have heard of, but many of you are familiar with the notorious serial killers such as; John Wayne Gacy, Jeffrey Dahmer, Ted Bundy, Gary Ridgway, Aileen Wuornos, and Dennis Rader, just to name a few. This reference book will make a great collection for true crime enthusiasts. Each story is in a Reader's Digest short form.

Backseat Tragedies: Hot Car Deaths
by JJ Slate and RJ Parker
April 15, 2015

Picture this: A mother parks her car in the parking lot of a supermarket and hops out to grab a few items. She'll only be gone a few minutes, so she leaves her baby in the backseat and cracks the front window. The child, too small to protest, doesn't even know what is happening. In a matter of minutes, the car begins to act like an oven. The lack of ventilation inside causes the temperature to increase twenty degrees for each ten minutes she is gone, even with a window slightly open. The child's cries remain unheard and fall silent once his body temperature reaches 107°F. How many infants and young children die each year due to the negligence of their parents? The answer is too many. No child deserves to die this way.

Our first reaction when we hear of another hot car death is to instinctively blame the parents. We think they must not be fit to be parents in the first place. Many are too obsessed with themselves that they forget what a selfless act it is to care for a child, while others just think of themselves as being too busy in their own lives than to worry about a child. But many incidents of hot car deaths are tragic accidents. It is difficult for many of us to comprehend, but parents can become distracted by today's on-the-go lifestyles and simply forget their child is in the backseat of the car.

Backseat Tragedies: Hot Car Deaths explores the circumstances that led to the deaths of several children who died of hyperthermia, or suffering a heatstroke in a car. We explain the facts about how quickly a car can heat to deadly temperatures and what steps you can take to prevent future tragedies. We hope to raise awareness about how a simple act of carelessness can result in the death of a beautiful child.

Please feel free to check out more TRUE
CRIME and CRIME FICTION books and authors
by our friends at

www.WILDBLUEPRESS.com

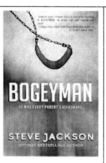
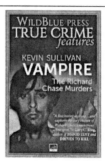

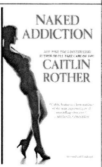

About the Author

RJ Parker, P.Mgr., CIM, is an award-winning and bestselling true crime author and serial killer expert. He has written 16 true crime books, available in eBook, trade paperback, and audiobook editions, that have sold in over 100 countries. He holds Certifications in Serial Crime and Criminal Profiling.

Parker publishes True CRIME and CRIME Fiction for several authors under his company, **RJ Parker Publishing, Inc.**

RJ Parker was born and raised in Mount Pearl, Newfoundland where he resides there and also in Toronto, Ontario. Parker started writing after becoming disabled with Anklyosing Spondylitis. He spent twenty-five years in various facets of Government and has two professional designations. In his spare time RJ enjoys playing the guitar, mandolin, piano, drums, steel guitar and sax. Many years ago he filled in several times with the rock bank April Wine, although Country music is his favorite.

As of December 2014, RJ has donated over 2,100 autographed books to allied troops serving overseas and to our **Wounded Warriors** recovering in Naval and Army hospitals all over the world. He also donates a percentage of royalties to **Victims of Violent Crimes**.

Contact Information

Facebook-
www.facebook.com/RJParkerPublishing
Email - AuthorRJParker@gmail.com
Email - Agent@RJParkerPublishing.com
Website - www.RJParkerPublishing.com
Twitter - @AuthorRJParker

References and Endnotes

[i] 2005 Serial Murder Symposium.
http://www.fbi.gov/stats-
services/publications/serial-murder
[ii] The Serial Killer Files – December, 2003
ISBN-13: 978-0345465665
[iii] Women Who Love Serial Killers by Dr.
  Katherine Ramsland
  http://www.psychologytoday.com/blog/shadow-
  boxing/201204/women-who-love-serial-
  killers/comments
[iv] Professor John Money
  http://nathanmaxwellcann.info/2010/02/10/hybri
  stophilia-bonnie-clyde-syndrome/
[v] Love Art History
  http://www.sciences360.com/index.php/hybristo
  philia-11178/
[vi] Women Who Love Men Who Kill - May 2000
  ISBN-13: 978-0595003990
[vii] Thanks to Sheriff Michael T. Downey -
  Humboldt County Police for answering many
  questions on the Wayne Adam Ford case.
[viii] Caroline Graham
  http://www.dailymail.co.uk/news/article-
  399234/The-actress-serial-killer.html

[ix] Radford Serial Killers Database
http://maamodt.asp.radford.edu/Psyc%20405/seri
al%20killers/Bundy,%20Ted%20-%202005.pdf

[x] Radford Serial Killers Database
http://maamodt.asp.radford.edu/Psyc%20405/seri
al%20killers/Ramirez,%20Richard%20_spring%
202007_.pdf

[xi] Ramsland, K. (n.d). The Night Stalker: Serial
Killer Richard Ramirez. Ramirez and Satan:
Perfect Together. Retrieved April 10, 2007, from
http://www.crimelibrary.com/serial_killers/notor
ious/ramirez/together_10.html

[xii] Jack Levin
http://www.sfgate.com/health/article/Killer-
groupies-an-unexplained-mystery-3215238.php

[xiii] Fab Magazine 2005
http://archive.fabmagazine.com/fabboy/archive/2
60/index.html#

[xiv] Canadian pycho Luka Magnotta Newsmaker of
the Year
http://news.nationalpost.com/2012/12/23/canadia
n-psycho-luka-magnotta-named-canadian-press-
newsmaker-of-the-year/

[xv] Crime Library Gerard Schaefer
http://www.crimelibrary.com/serial_killers/preda
tors/gerard_schaefer/7.html

[xvi] Radford Serial Killers Database
http://maamodt.asp.radford.edu/Psyc%20405/seri
al%20killers/Rolling,%20Danny%20-
%202004.pdf

[xvii] Philpin, J. & Donnelly, J. (1994). Beyond
Murder: The Inside Account of the Gainesville
Student Murders. NY: Penguin Books.

[xviii] London, S. & Rolling, D. (1996) *The Making of
A Serial Killer: The Real Story of the Gainsville
Murders in the Killer's Own Words*. Portland:
Feral House.

[xix] Radford Serial Killers Database
http://maamodt.asp.radford.edu/Psyc%20405/seri
al%20killers/Bianchi,%20Kenneth.pdf

[xx] Radford Serial Killers Database
http://maamodt.asp.radford.edu/Psyc%20405/seri
al%20killers/Buono,%20Angelo.pdf

[xxi] O'Brien, Darcy. (1985). Two of a Kind: The
Hillside Stranglers. New York: New American
Library

[xxii] Doug Clark - Biography
http://en.wikipedia.org/wiki/Doug_Clark

[xxiii] Carol Bundy - Biography
http://en.wikipedia.org/wiki/Carol_M._Bundy

[xxiv] Schmid, David (2006). Natural Born Celebrities: Serial Killers in American Culture. University of Chicago Press

[xxv] Flowers, R. Barri. *Serial Killer Couples: Bonded by Sexual Depravity, Abduction, and Murder*

[xxvi] Frank Colistro http://www.kptv.com/story/21352713/serial-killer-groupies

[xxvii] www.writeaprisoner.com

CPSIA information can be obtained at www.ICGtesting.com
Printed in the USA
LVOW10s1942120615

442295LV00019B/148/P